JMBennett.
JULY 1977.

North British Album

Title page: The massive girders of the Forth Bridge form a magnificent backcloth to Glen class 4-4-0 No 62492 *Glen Garvin* as it hastens a northbound local train from Edinburgh to Fife. The train is rather a motley collection of rolling stock, emanating from both LMS and LNER sources./*E. R. Wethersett*

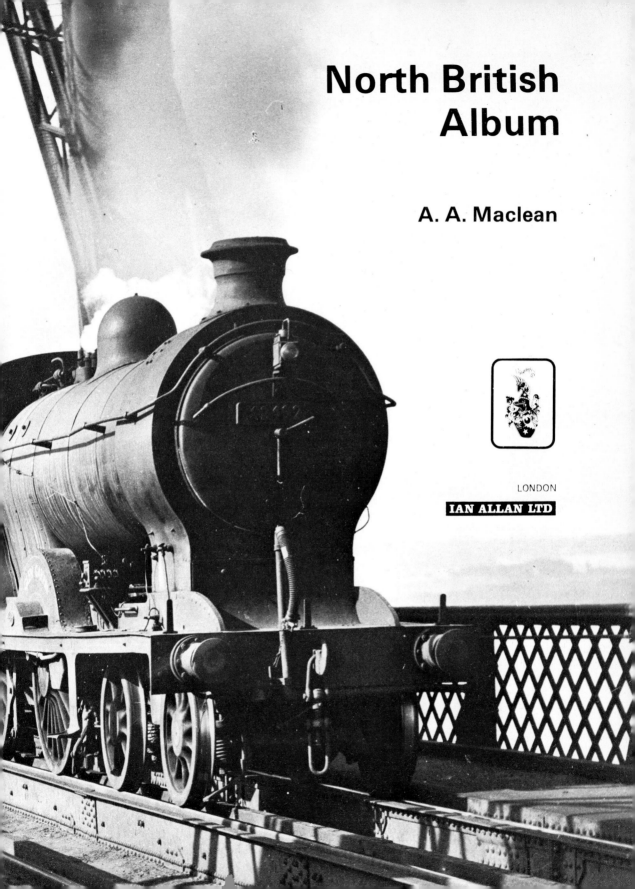

North British Album

A. A. Maclean

LONDON

IAN ALLAN LTD

First published 1975

ISBN 0 7110 0568 0

Published by Ian Allan Ltd, Shepperton, Surrey
and printed in the United Kingdom by
Ian Allan (Printing) Ltd.

Colour Frontispiece and Jacket: Under the shadow of Ben More, a Glasgow (Queen Street) to Fort William train leaves Crianlarich hauled by 4-4-0 No 406 *Glen Croe.* These engines, with 6ft coupled wheels, were specially designed by Reid to work over the heavily graded West Highland Line./*Painting by George Heiron*

Acknowledgements

In the compilation of this work I have received very valuable assistance from many sources, and I would like to take this opportunity of expressing my appreciation. Among those who have placed their collections at my disposal must be mentioned Messrs C. L. Kerr, W. S. Sellar, W. A. C. Smith, J. Bryant and P. Westwater. Others who have made invaluable contributions include D. Martin, J. Hay, G. Barbour and the staff of the Scottish Record Office, Messrs Yerbury of Edinburgh, and lastly but by no means least, the PR & PO of the Scottish Region of British Rail. To the other contributors, whose names receive credit in the text, I would also express thanks.

Smokebox view of Atlantic type locomotive No.875 *Midlothian.* Withdrawn in December 1937, this engine was reinstated in traffic on the following June, pending preservation in the LNER Museum at York, but wartime conditions intervened and the engine was ultimately withdrawn for breaking up at the close of 1939./ *British Railways*

The North British Railway Company

At 7 am on the morning of Monday June 22nd, 1846, a passenger train hauled by motive power built in Newcastle on Tyne and comprising coaching stock built in Edinburgh departed from the small station at Berwick upon Tweed and headed northwards to the Scottish Capital. This was the first Anglo-Scottish passenger train and its operation heralded the official opening of the North British Railway which was to give a further 77 years of service to the community as an independent entity.

Although this was not the first North British Railway train, (these had nominally been operating since the Edinburgh & Dalkeith Railway was absorbed by the North British in 1845), it forms a convenient starting point from which to outline the development of the company which, by the grouping of 1923 was to rank as the fifth largest in Britain, with a route mileage of almost 1,378. It was, of course, the largest of the Scottish Railways, its nearest contender being the age-old rival, the Caledonian with almost 1,115 route miles.

Geographically within Scotland, the NB was to achieve complete monopoly of the counties of Berwickshire, Haddingtonshire, Selkirkshire, Fife and Kinross-shire. It was also to encompass within its boundaries the most westerly station in Great Britain — Arisaig — between Fort William and Mallaig on the West Highland Railway. The northermost point to which the North British owned its own metals on the East Coast was at Bervie, later renamed Inverbervie, north of Montrose, although this was reached by passing over the Dundee & Arbroath Joint Line which it partnered with the Caledonian. Aberdeen was reached by passing over the Caley northwards from the famous Kinnaber Junction, focal point of the late 19th Century Races to the North. It is of interest at this point to observe that whereas the NB on its run from Berwick to Aberdeen passed over the Caley metals, the latter company also required running powers over the East Coast Company for a short distance in the Coatbridge area where the rails of the old Monklands Railway were used to effect a through route from Carlisle to Aberdeen.

Although the line was Scottish based, this did not prevent it making large inroads into the north of England and considerable mileages were owned and operated in Northumberland and Cumberland, mainly by the absorption or the promotion of smaller independent railway companies.

One of the main difficulties which faced the North British in its early days was the difference in gauge which existed between itself and the horse-drawn Edinburgh & Dalkeith Railway, thus precluding immediate running over both systems. This disadvantage was considered to be considerably outweighed by the advantage of having a line pointing in the general direction of Carlisle. It had been the intention of the North British to acquire a monopoly for itself in a triangle bounded by Edinburgh, Berwick and Carlisle, and in this it was to be singularly successful.

After the opening of the Berwick line, attention was then turned to the direction of Carlisle, and although Hawick was reached on November 1st, 1849, it was to be a further ten years before the line providing the link received authorisation, and that in the face of proposals with Caledonian backing from the Carlisle end. Eventually the line was opened throughout on July 1st, 1862, access to Carlisle being achieved by using the running

The North British Railway company's coat of arms./ E. Catchpool

6

powers inherited with the Port Carlisle Railway, over the Caledonian Railway from what was to become Carlisle No 3 Junction into Citadel Station. Like the Edinburgh & Hawick, the Hawick-Carlisle section was opened in stages, but from the Carlisle end.

In the interim, the Border Counties Railway, which left the Carlisle line at the isolated village of Riccarton, was built to a junction with the Newcastle & Carlisle Railway near Hexham, and running powers were obtained by the North British to Newcastle over the North Eastern, who had absorbed the N&C, but at the expense of giving the English railway running powers into Edinburgh from Berwick, a move which was later to give deep grounds for regret when the North Eastern virtually was to oust the NB from its own line in the running of Anglo-Scottish services.

The North Eastern Railway had a branch line from Tweedmouth which ran westwards to Sprouston Junction, also known as Mellendean Junction after a nearby farm, where an end-on connection was made with the North British Kelso-St Boswells branch, in June 1851. The opening of the Royal Border Bridge at Berwick almost a year earlier, in August 1850, now gave the NB alternative routes to Newcastle, which were to be invaluable in later years.

August 1st, 1862 witnessed the first of the two basic amalgamations which were ultimately to shape the final form of the Company. On that date the NB and the Edinburgh, Perth and Dundee Railway Company came together, and some brief notes on the latter line are not amiss.

The EP&D was originally conceived as the Edinburgh & Northern Railway, to operate from Burntisland to Perth and Ferry-Port-on-Craig, from which latter point steamer services were operated to Broughty Ferry for Dundee. Authorised in 1845, the line officially opened to public traffic on September 20th, 1847 when a restricted service was provided from Burntisland, but this only extended as far as Cupar on the Tayport line and Lindores on the Perth branch. However, to reach Edinburgh, it had acquired the small Edinburgh, Leith and Granton Railway in 1847. The Edinburgh Leith and Granton operated partly by steam and partly by stationary beam engine, trains being drawn up the incline from the General Station in Edinburgh to Scotland Street, through a tunnel over its entire length. In Fife, the Edinburgh & Northern used the same method of working for the Kirkcaldy Harbour Branch where the ruling grade is 1 in 23.

As will have been noted, the Edinburgh & Northern Railway was rather fragmented in that a traveller from Edinburgh to Dundee would require to use three trains and two steamers to achieve his destination, the two gaps from Lindores and Cupar to Perth and Tayport respectively being closed in mid 1848. A major branch line, from Thornton to Dunfermline was also near completion at that time, but delay was experienced in obtaining authority to cross the Halbeath Tramway. This was finally overcome by taking out three separate Bills, (one to go over, one to go under and one to cross on the level) and against opposition from the tramway proprietors, one was successful and the gap was closed, opening the line in December 1849, by which time the Edinburgh & Northern had changed its name to the 'Edinburgh, Perth and Dundee Railway Company'.

The first train ferry in the world, the Leviathan, was put into service at Tayport, but was considered better suited to the Firth of Forth conditions and subsequently transferred to Burntisland, where she was to be joined by sister vessels to convey vehicles across the river until the opening of the Forth Bridge in 1890. It is of interest that the maintenance of the steamer fleet, whether on Tay or Forth crossings, was in the hands of the railway workshops of the EP&D at Burntisland. It is doubtful if there was any other place in Britain where railway locomotive works maintained steamships!

At Dunfermline, an end-on connection was made with the Stirling & Dunfermline Railway and from August 1850, the latter line was operated to Alloa, using EP&D stock, ostensibly on loan, as the line was claimed to be an offspring of the Edinburgh & Glasgow Railway Company (to which it was not physically connected).

As was the case with the North British Railway, the EP&D continued to expand its operational mileage by working agreements and amalgamations. In the former category can be included the St Andrews Railway (opened July 1st, 1852) where the smaller line was in the entire operational hands of the larger concern, and the Leven Railway (opened July 3rd, 1854) where the constituent was required to provide a locomotive of its own, the remainder of stock being supplied by the EP&D. The Kinross-shire Railway, linking Kinross with Lumphinnans Jct, between Cowdenbeath and Lochgelly came to the EP&D by an Act of July 1861, and the Fife and Kinross was amalgamated from July 29th, 1862, only a few days before the larger line was itself taken over by the North British.

The Leven Railway, which had been regarded by E&N as an upstart, amalgamated with the line between Leven and Kilconquhar (6ml 57ch) which was grandly termed the 'East of Fife Railway' and the two concerns, known as the Leven & East Fife Railway were to expand their original objectives by reaching Anstruther before coming under the NB 'umbrella' in 1877.

Before passing on, it is interesting to record that the old Edinburgh & Northern Railway Company became one of the few rail concerns to present a medal to a road passenger undertaking, but in recognition of effecting great improvements in transportation facilities in Fife, a Mr McNab, of Cupar, was the recipient. Before Mr McNab's efforts, transport in Fife was by a two horse diligence between Newport and Kinghorn, with a wait of what could extend to two to three days at the Inn at Pettycur for the weather to make a sailing feasable, to Edinburgh. McNab introduced a four horse diligence and greatly improved the ferry, and showed that the Firth could be crossed at every state of the tide and wind. It was apparently considered by the railway company that Mr McNab was instrumental in creating a travel market within the county, from which, needless to say, the railway benefited.

To the west of Edinburgh lay the Edinburgh & Glasgow Railway which was instituted in 1838 and opened to passenger traffic on February 22nd, 1842. The actual route had been predetermined by three English engineers who placed the consideration of gradients and convenience for north bound connections before

ROAD TRANSPORT

The North British operated this one horse power omnibus between the station at Mussleburgh, near Edinburgh, through the streets to a premises known as 'Formans Public House'. As can be observed from the advertisement on the 'decency boards', through bookings could be made to Edinburgh, 1st and 2nd class passengers being charged 10d and 8d respectively and permitted to sit inside, the 3rd class community being charged 5d and requiring to brave the elements. Non rail passengers were also catered for at 2d inside and 1d outside! Although the guard sports railway uniform, the driver certainly does not. The North British carried its road borne freight by agreements with local contractors using the latter's equipment. It is interesting to note that 1856 saw the old E&G using Pickfords./E. R. Yerbury

THROUGH FARES TO EDINBURGH.
1st Class Rail 10d 2nd Class Rail 8d
and Inside Coach. and Inside Coach.

NORTH BRITISH RAILWAY COMPANY.

9

brevity of distance. Only at the Glasgow end, where it had been the intention to take the line over the Union Canal into a high level terminus, was trouble encountered, in that the proprietors of the canal, wishing to link with the Monkland Canal to form a route for ocean going vessels across central Scotland vetoed the scheme. Such was the influence of the canals at that time, that the railway deferred to them and were faced with the burden of the Cowlairs Incline into the Glasgow terminus. Originally worked by hemp rope, a stronger material was soon in use and the beam engine at the summit was not displaced by conventional motive power until November 1908. At the eastern end of the line, the original terminus was at Haymarket, then on the outskirts of the city, and mileages were indicated by road type mileposts, with a total distance of 46 miles. Many of these are still in use to-day. The extension to Edinburgh Waverley, which raised the route miles to 47¼ was brought into use in 1846.

The development of the E&G is no different from that of its contemporaries and in addition to the main line between the two cities, only some 5½ miles is attributable to an Act under its own name. This is the line from Campsie Junction (now Lenzie) to Lennoxtown and Kirkintilloch for which powers were obtained in 1845, the line being opened three years later. The Edinburgh & Bathgate Railway leaves the main line to the west of Ratho station. August 3rd, 1846 was the date of authorisation, and it was leased to the E&G for 999 years from January 1st, 1852. When the NB amalgamated with the E&G in 1865 the lease was altered to run for 982 years to the new owner. Legally, the line remained independent until the passing of the 1921 Act, when it became part of the LNER. The Stirlingshire Midland Junction Railway was authorised by Act of 1846 and opened between Polmont & Larbert in September 1850. During the life of the SMJ, the option was left open to the Edinburgh & Glasgow Railway to undertake the construction work. The Stirling & Dunfermline Railway has already been mentioned under the Edinburgh & Northern Railway, but this line, with the branches to Tillicoultry and Alloa Harbour was incorporated in July 1846, the Edinburgh & Glasgow Railway agreeing to take over the line. In 1849, the E&G declined to fulfil their obligation on the grounds that the conditions of the amalgamation had not been effected by the S&D, the Scottish Central having obtained powers to stop the S&D going to

Stirling and erecting a station there. In 1853, the House of Lords to whom the dispute had gone, found that the E&G/S&D agreement was in fact binding, the lease being backdated to the date of the completion of the Dunfermline — Alloa portion (September 4th, 1850). The S&D then extended their line to Gas Works, Stirling, and when challenged by the Scottish Central the matter was legally resolved in favour of the Edinburgh & Glasgow. The subsequent disputes between the Edinburgh & Glasgow and the Scottish Central were resolved by Act of June 1858, when the entire line was vested in the former company's name. The Caledonian & Dumbartonshire Junction Railway and the Glasgow, Dumbarton & Helensburgh Railway dating from incorporation in 1846 and 1855 respectively, came into the Edinburgh & Glasgow fold in 1862. The little Alva Railway was amalgamated by Act of 1863, the E&G purchasing the line and assuming the debt.

The irony of the reason for the construction of the Cowlairs Incline — strong opposition from the Union Canal Company — was brought home seven years later, when the Union Canal was forced by economic circumstances to amalgamate with the Edinburgh & Glasgow Railway, the E&G assuming the debt of the Canal Company of £95,000.

Before the amalgamation of the E&G with the NB the former had a line under construction from Queensferry Junction, near Ratho, via Kirkliston to South Queensferry, but this line was not opened until 1866.

Apart from extensions and amalgamations, the chief points of interest with the Edinburgh & Glasgow lies with its relations with the Scottish Central and the Caledonian Railways. The Caledonian and the Scottish Central always had an understanding of sorts that one day they would be one, but the E&G, who had aspirations of striking northwards from Greenhill also wooed the common ground. In 1848, an agreement was made with the LNW, CR, SCR, and E&GR for traffic division, but this was broken off and competition for the inter-city trade was renewed. In 1853, the CR and E&GR came under joint management, but after unsuccessfully attempting to obtain parliamentary backing, the arrangement was terminated in July 1854. A cut price war was then waged, but proved so disastrous that an agreement was entered into in February 1856, which was to last for ten years. The E&G proportion was 30.64 per cent, the CR taking

69.36 per cent. This agreement continued until August 1st, 1864, when a working agreement with the NB was introduced. The SCR was admitted into the 'common purse' agreement in 1860, and a Bill was proposed for amalgamation of the three concerns in 1861, but this was rejected. It was put forward again in 1861, and again in 1864, but was defeated on both occasions.

Prior to coming under North British control, the Edinburgh & Glasgow joined forces with the Monkland Railways, which was the result of an amalgamation in 1848 of the Monkland & Kirkintilloch Railway of 1826, the Ballochney Railway of 1828, (which was in effect an extension of the M&K), and the Slamannan Railway of 1841, which extended the Ballochney across Central Scotland, to Causewayend, near Manuel. The Slamannan & Borrowstouness Act of 1846 gave the complex access to the east coast on the Firth of Forth at Bo'ness.

The Monkland & Kirkintilloch Railway took delivery on its 4ft 6in gauge in 1831 of two steam locomotives from Murdoch Aitken & Company of Glasgow. They were the first two steam engines built in Scotland, and if one passes over a claim from the Kilmarnock & Troon, a horse operated line on the west coast, to have tried this propulsion, they were the first steam locomotives to work in Scotland. The Ballochney Railway harnessed the forces of gravity to operate a distance of some 1,100 yards near Coatbridge, where, taking an advantage of the fact that loaded traffic was mainly unidirectional, descending vehicles pulled up empty wagons, the ruling gradient being 1 in 23. Operation was governed by horizontal pulleys at the summit, and for some of the distance, interlaced track with a common rail was used. Not far from the foot of the gradient was located the Kipps Works of the Monkland, the name deriving from a sunken track at Incline Top known as a 'Kip.' In later years, vehicles descending the incline were controlled by the brake wagons of the type used on the Cowlairs Incline in Glasgow.

Before returning to the North British, it is of interest to recall that the directorate of the Edinburgh & Glasgow Railway consented to the construction of houses for rental to the staff in the vicinity of Cowlairs. Four tenements were erected, accommodation being provided for 143 families. Rentals varied, according to the size of the flat, but these ranged from £6 to £20 per annum. The structures survived until the late 1950s when they were demolished, having out-lived their usefulness with the development of amenities provided by corporations.

August 1st, 1865 was the first day when the combined strength of the various constituent companies functioned as one entity — on paper at least. Three main workshops existed — Cowlairs (Glasgow), St Margarets (Edinburgh) and Burntisland (Fife) — each geared to cope with the demands of their respective lines, but it was Cowlairs which was to emerge as the main mechanical centre for the enlarged concern, the others becoming strategic repair points, as did Kipps. Processes of amalgamations had left the North British with a motley collection of plant — some of which only existed on paper — and some degree of rationalisation was essential. The NB was to be fortunate in having men capable of fulfilling this function and the date of amalgamation can be said to have been the starting point of a new era.

The total mileage of the combined organisations amounted to some 75 per cent of the total finally achieved by the North British before it lost its separate identity in the Grouping under the 1921 Transport Act. Most of the trunk lines had already been constructed, perhaps the most noticeable exception being the West Highland Railway from Craigendoran to Mallaig, a distance of some 142 miles. In both Glasgow and Edinburgh, local suburban services were still to develop their full potential. In Edinburgh, the line through the Scotland Street Tunnel was closed with the opening of a line permitting through running from Waverley to Granton and Leith via Abbeyhill. The tunnel was not, however, left to decay, and since March 1868, has been used for mushroom cultivation, an air raid shelter, an emergency control room and a garage for motor cars!

1871 was the year in which Thomas Wheatley introduced the inside cylinder 4-4-0 to the British railway scene. Two machines formed this inaugural class, one of which was to achieve notoriety in that it was the locomotive which hauled the ill fated train which plunged to the bed of the Firth of Tay on December 28th, 1879. Raised from the water, it was to be restored to traffic and later rebuilt as a compound for two years to the Nisbet system. Rebuilt later by Holmes, 224, as she was numbered, survived until 1919.

1873 saw the introduction, by the North British of all lines, to the public of the sleeping car. A six wheeler, designed and built by Ashbury, the car entered service between Glasgow & Kings Cross (London), but was not an unqualified success. The NB ultimately transferred it to East Coast Joint Stock in 1875.

The Midland Railway commenced running of through trains to Glasgow and Edinburgh in 1876, and the NB 'Waverley' route was transformed from a rural branch to part of a main trunk route. Special vehicles were allocated to the service and designated 'Midland Scottish Joint Stock', and this resulted in the construction at Cowlairs of very Midland design carriages. After the construction of new vehicles for this service in 1905/6, the NB took over a number of the old MSJS cars and turned them out in the NB standard livery.

August 1st, 1876, saw the amalgamation of the Peebles Railway into the NB fold. This line had been leased to the major concern since 1861 and as such was the first constituent line to contribute locomotives to stock.

General expansion of the system continued apace, 1880 seeing the North British becoming a partner with the Caledonian Railway in the Dundee and Arbroath line, although the gap of the Tay prevented through working at that time. The same year saw the completion of the line between Arbroath and Kinnaber Junction, the Montrose and Bervie Railway coming under the NB by Act of August 1881, although the line had been opened since 1865. The only gaps on the main line to the north now lay in the two Firths, although this was in hand for early attention.

During the short period in which it had been operational, the first Tay Viaduct had so proved itself to the North British Board that powers were obtained for the erection of a new structure in 1881, linking the existing lines between Wormit and Dundee, although slightly upstream of the predecessor. On the Forth, work on the Bouch designed bridge ceased after the Tay accident, and a new Act was passed in 1882 for a stronger structure to the design of Barlow, on the cantilever principle. The new Tay Viaduct opened in 1887, followed three years later by the Forth Bridge.

During the time that these two giant civil engineering works were being progressed, the suburban railway networks in both Glasgow and Edinburgh were being enlarged, in the former by the construction of the Glasgow, Yoker and Clydebank Railway opened in 1882, and in the east by the Edinburgh Suburban and South Side

Junction Railway, opened in 1884. The Glasgow City and District Railway, linking College and Kelvinhaugh opened in 1886 and gave the citizens of Glasgow a taste of a steam worked underground line.

The last decade of the 19th Century was marked, in NB terms, by the building of the famous West Highland Railway, northwards from Craigendoran to Fort William. Opened in 1894, this line was perhaps endowed with a distinctive individuality in that special locomotives and rolling stock were designed for it, the station buildings bearing a stronger affinity with Switzerland than with Scotland. Worked by the NB from the outset, it remained legally independent until 1908.

Although the Forth Bridge had required a large amount of new trackwork leading to and from it, such was the growth of traffic that it was found that the existing facilities were being severely strained to cope. This certainly applied to the Waverley Station, and reconstruction on a massive scale was put in hand in 1892 and to conclusion, including the North British Hotel took some ten years. Lines were quadrupled to the west as far as Saughton, and new tunnels were built to carry the widened lines into and through Princes Street Gardens.

The Light Railway Order Act of 1898 facilitated the construction of the line from Fountainhall Junction on the 'Waverely Route' to Oxton and Lauder, and when opened in 1901, this section had the distinction of being the first line in Scotland to be authorised under the Act. 1901 also saw the opening of the Ormiston — Gifford and Banavie — Mallaig lines.

By the close of 1901, the North British .had achieved most of the mileage which it was to possess at 1923, the main additions being the Kincardine — Dunfermline (1906), and the Spean Bridge to Fort Augustus line which came to the NB in 1907, was closed in 1911, and re-opened in 1913. The line was bought outright by the North British in 1914.

Competition with the Caledonian for traffic on the Aberdeen routes from both Glasgow and Edinburgh was the spur which was to affect the traditional design pattern both for locomotives and carriages in 1906. From the Glasgow works of the North British Locomotive Company were delivered the first of the only Atlantic type locomotives to be operated by a Scottish company. From the NB works at Cowlairs came the first of a series of carriages with an entirely new profile which was to become the North British standard during the remainder of that Company's existence, for new construction.

In November 1908, a link with the earliest days of the old Edinburgh & Glasgow Railway was broken with the discontinuance of cable haulage on the Cowlairs incline. The stone structure which housed the old stationery engine at the summit was to survive for a further half century, although rebuilt internally to house electrical equipment for the Works across the line.

In September 1913, the North British followed the example of the Midland Railway in England and adopted the centralised 'control' system of train regulation. Initially established at Portobello, near Edinburgh, this was later reorganised in the light of experience, and moved to Waverley Station, from which centre it still operates. In the west, a similar organisation was established at Coatbridge, and for the Fife and Dundee Area, Burntisland was selected, although this latter location did not become effective until 1920.

A completely revised system of locomotive classification was introduced to co-ordinate with the Controls, freight locomotives being grouped in classes accorded letters 'A' to 'G', passenger locomotives being given 'H' to 'R', both ostensibly in descending order of power. There were some exceptions to the rule, and the large varient of 6-coupled goods locomotives, originally 'B' was reclassed when boiler pressure was increased, to follow the passenger engines as Class 'S'.

During World War 1, the North British Railway with headquarters in Edinburgh acted as 'Secretary Company' to the Scottish Railway network on behalf of Scottish Command at Edinburgh Castle. Wartime traffic was to severely tax the resources of the line, many wartime camps and bases being established along its lines of routes. The opening for freight traffic in 1915 of the group of lines in the Niddrie/Portobello/Monktonhall area near Edinburgh, collectively called 'The Lothian Lines' greatly relieved the traffic situation at the eastern approaches to the city. These lines were not, however, a result of the war, the Act authorising construction being achieved in 1913.

After the cessation of hostilities, the NB was to successfully press a claim against the Government of the day for compensation, but legal expenses presented quite a drain on the Railway's financial position, particularly so when heavy accumulated arrears of maintenance and new construction were being dealt with.

In 1921, with the passing of the Railways Act, the future of the North British Railway Company as a separate entity was no longer in doubt, and as a result, plans for renewals and construction of rolling stock were quietly dropped, although locomotive construction was to continue at Cowlairs until 1924 when the final engine, by then classed 'N.15' by the new Company, the London & North Eastern, was turned out. It is of interest to note that this design was originally produced for work on the Cowlairs Incline, the very first Cowlairs product being destined for the same task some 80 years before.

When the full influence of the new concern came to pass, all stock appeared in LNER livery, with the exception of the Clyde steamers which remained in NB colours, although under a different house flag, until 1936.

The name of the North British Railway Company which had survived unaltered through several amalgamations, and indeed threatened amalgamations such as with the Caledonian and later the Glasgow & South Western Railways which did not come to pass, was at last forced to recede into the pages of history, and somehow the term 'Southern Scottish Area' never quite seemed to fit the bill. Twenty-five years later, the name of the London & North Eastern Railway was itself to give way under the 1947 Transport Act to the all embracing title of 'British Railways'. Perhaps the prophetic statement made in the last decade of the 19th Century that the North British Railway would someday expand and require to drop the 'North' from its title had indeed come true!

North British Railway

WAVERLEY STATION

These two views depict the stations at Wavereley Bridge, Edinburgh in the early 1850s.

Below: This view, from the vicinity of the Scott Monument, depicts the original facades. The large building in the centre served both the North British and Edinburgh & Glasgow Railway Companies, the smaller building on the left being for the Edinburgh Perth & Dundee Railway. In both instances steps led down to platform level. In the background are multi-storey tenement blocks — many of which are still extant.

Bottom: The panorama is entirely different, looking across the 'train shed' to the new town, with on the right, the EP&D station with some rolling stock. This station was at right angles to the Joint Station, but connecting lines facilitated interchange. On the left is the goods station of the Edinburgh & Glasgow Railway. The building to the rear of the main EPDR building was the station refreshment rooms, later converted to NBR offices./*E. R. Yerbury*

WAVERLEY EAST (1854)

Above: The approaches to the General Station at Edinburgh from the south are depicted in this print, the original of which dates from 1854. Although much of the rolling stock is liable to be of original designs, some types bear a strong resemblance to those of half a century later. The signal tower, surmounted by a disc and crossbar signal can be noted in the right centreground. This was to remain operational for a further decade, when 'space interval' superceded the 'time interval' method of working, and a new building, known as the 'New Observatory' was commissioned for controlling trains./*Edinburgh Public Libraries*

WAVERLEY EAST (1875)

Below: This view, from the same vantage point as that on the previous photograph, clearly depicts the growth in passenger traffic, although it must be borne in mind that the freight traffic had been moved to the south side of the station, in effect enlarging the site of the Edinburgh & Glasgow Railway premises. The rolling stock dates the picture, with the then new 'Ashbury' designs mixing with constituent lines carriages./*Aberdeen University Library*

WAVERLEY WEST

These views depict the development at the western end of the station, necessitated by the growth in traffic over the period 1862-1872.

Above: The view, from the ground below the Scott Monument, shows the portion of line between the Waverley Bridge (left) and the Mound Tunnel as it appeared in 1862, three years before the E&G and the NB amalgamated. The arches under the Waverley Bridge led to the joint station, and smaller arches were built under the large ones for extra support./*E. R. Yerbury Collection*

Below: In this illustration, platforms have been extended and the bridge of stone has given way to steel. As in the upper print, most of the stock is of Edinburgh & Glasgow Railway origin./*Aberdeen University Library*

NB HOTEL, EDINBURGH

Below: The buildings in this illustration have an interesting history in that they were erected in 1771-1776, before the railway age, without the consent of the feuers, and were the subject of an acrimonious dispute between the Town Council and the feuers of the New Town. It was finally agreed in 1776 that the houses already built should remain, but no further construction should take place west of what was to become the railway offices. Located within the same block were three hotels, a refreshment room suite, photographers' premises and of course the railway companies whose advertisements can be seen in the picture. The buildings were pulled down to make way for the present North British Hotel, opened on October 16th, 1902 at a cost of £221,000, but adhering to the same territorial limits. The area in the immediate foreground, with the floral display, is the roof of the Waverley Market, built on the site of the former Edinburgh, Perth and Dundee Railway Terminus, and demolished in 1973./*E. R. Yerbury*

NB STATION, ALLOA

Bottom: Rolling stock occupies most of the available track space in this early illustration of the station at Alloa, outpost of the Edinburgh & Glasgow Railway. The date is 1860./*G. Cumming*

VINTAGE POWER

Cowlairs Works provides the backcloth for this workstained 2-4-0 which carries the combined ownership and numberplate of Edinburgh & Glasgow Railway No 9. The absence of brakeblocks on the engine is interesting, presumably being compensated for to a degree by the tender fittings. The date is 1860./*Author's Collection*

Against a background of contemporary advertising, 0-4-2ST No 1080 propels vehicles into the old goods station at Glasgow Queen Street. Built in 1866 as an 0-4-2 tender engine from parts of old engines, this locomotive was rebuilt into the form illustrated in 1888. It was to survive until 1907./*Photomatic Ltd*

Standing in the eastern approaches to Waverley Station is 2-2-2 No 213. Originally built to Charles Beyer's design for the E&GR in 1856, she was rebuilt twice by Wheatley and once by Holmes, being renumbered no less than four times before her demise in 1909. The poor external finish would appear to indicate that a visit to works was called for!/*BR*

No 63, a somewhat austere looking 2-4-0, is claimed to have had origins in a Hawthorn machine of 1851, parts of which were incorporated into the locomotive illustrated. It is, however, perhaps fairer to describe the engine as having been built in 1873 at Cowlairs. Renumbered on three occasions during her life, she ended her days on the South Leith Branch near Edinburgh, as No 1029 in 1903./ *Locomotive Publishing Co*

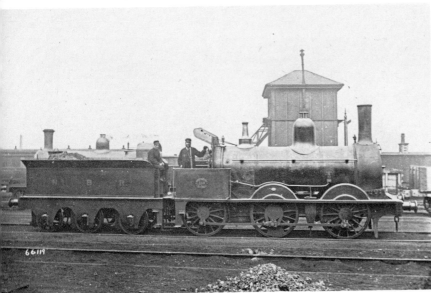

Burntisland Works was the birthplace of this 0-6-0. Laid down under the auspices of the Edinburgh, Perth and Dundee Railway, the amalgamation of that line with the NB occurred before completion and she emerged as a North British Railway locomotive, in 1863. She was not destined to have a long life, being withdrawn as the last of her class in 1896. Here depicted as No 159A, her final numbering was to be 863./ *LPC*

Sharp Brothers provided the Edinburgh & Glasgow Railway Company with two similar 2-4-0 locomotives in 1854, both of which were subsequently rebuilt by the North British Railway. No 231, illustrated here after being 'duplicated' as 231A, was to survive its sister by three years, being broken up in 1894. The constructional methods employed in the tender are well depicted in the illustration./ *Author's Collection*

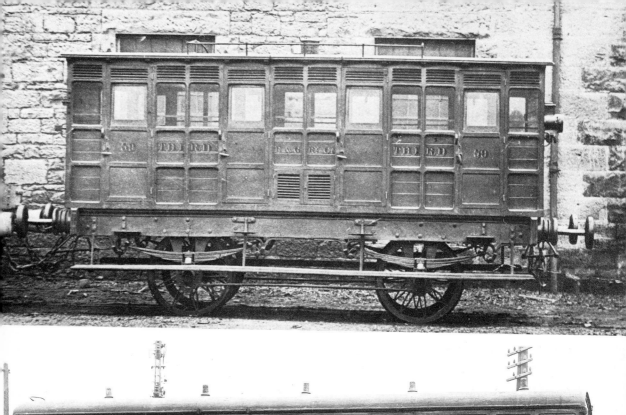

COACHING STOCK—FOUR WHEEL

Top: No 59 was built for the Edinburgh & Glasgow Railway Company and is depicted here in the varnished wood condition of the early 1860s. Worthy of note is the absence of brake gear, the dog box, indicated by the louvres in the lower centre of the bodywork, and the rather large tail lamp./*A Maclean Collection*

Above: The four wheel passenger carriage continued in construction until the mid 1890s although the six wheeler and to a small extent the bogie vehicle had been in production for some time at that stage. No 1072 is a Cowlairs product of 1890, and portrays the final design of passenger carrying NB four wheeler./ *BR*

COACHING STOCK — SIX WHEEL

Top: The six wheel carriage was to a large extent an extended four wheeler, but the additional length resulted in a much larger number of different types. One of these, the centre brake third, is represented by No 1145 seen here in LNER numbering and livery. Apart from the addition of vacuum brake fittings, the vehicle is in NB condition. */Courtesy A. G. Dunbar*

Above: 1893 was the date of construction of 32379, which was originally NBR No 112 in the Composite series. This vehicle was fitted with no fewer than four lavatories, each with the NB coat of arms etched into the glass. An early form of Standard design, many were converted into thirds, and saloons as the need arose. The basic design became extinct early in 1938. */Courtesy W. T. Stubbs*

COACHING STOCK — EIGHT WHEEL

Top left: The first North British bogie carriages emerged from Cowlairs in 1889, but with the exception of some special types, such as the 1894 West Highland stock, large scale production did not commence until 1902. These cars, like their 1889 predecessors were merely enlarged six-wheelers. No 1730 illustrates this, and was one of a large class, which although lavatory fitted were not vestibuled. Built in 1904, this coach lasted in service until June 1952.

Centre left: With the advent of the 'Aberdeen Block Trains' of 1906, came the basic outline and dimensions which was to become standard for nearly all new NB construction. No 1793, which carries the named train board for the 'Fife Coast Express', represents the main line corridor type.

Bottom left: Suburban non corridor carriages produced after 1906 were similar to the vestibuled stock. No 127, built in 1910 and fitted out originally with gas lighting, represents the final development of the type. On withdrawal from service in February 1953, this car entered departmental service and was renumbered DE320209./*BR*

DINING CARRIAGES

Top: Contrary to popular belief, the first North British Railway dining carriages were not the all steel 'Craven' types of 1919, but two twelve wheel designs which emerged almost simultaneously from Cowlairs in 1907. No 250 illustrates the 66ft 0¾in long vehicle, the kitchen accommodation being in the third and fourth compartments from the left, meals being served at individual compartments. Before the 1923 grouping, the kitchen space had been converted into a lounge. Somewhat uniquely for North British coaches, they carried the NBR monogram in addition to the normal crests./*BR*

Above: No 162 was a former East Coast Joint Stock Composite Dining Carriage built at Doncaster in 1905 and purchased in 1913. Originally ECJS No 196, this was one of two similar vehicles purchased at that time the other becoming NB No 163 (ECJS 353). Both cars passed to the LNER and were to be renumbered 32429 and 32430 respectively./*BR*

23

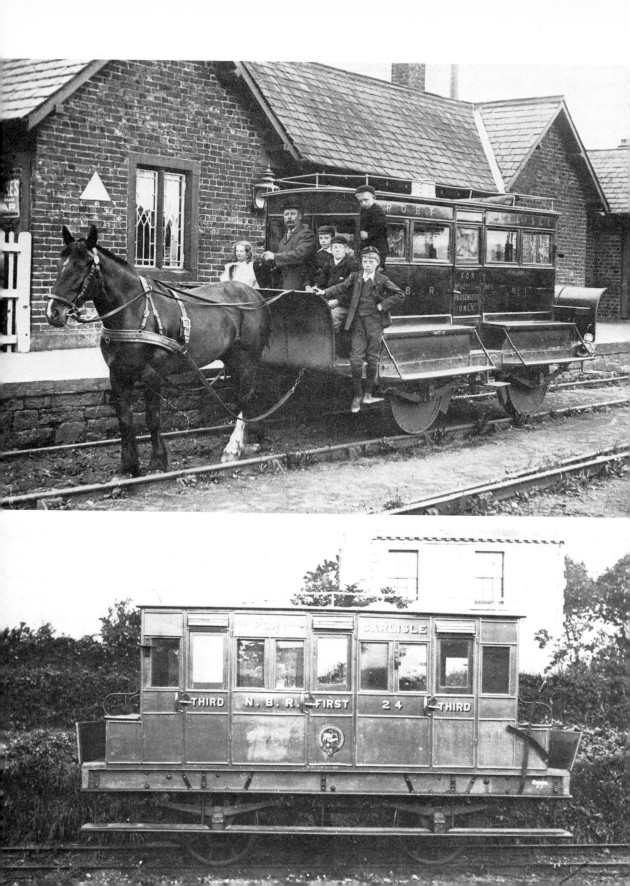

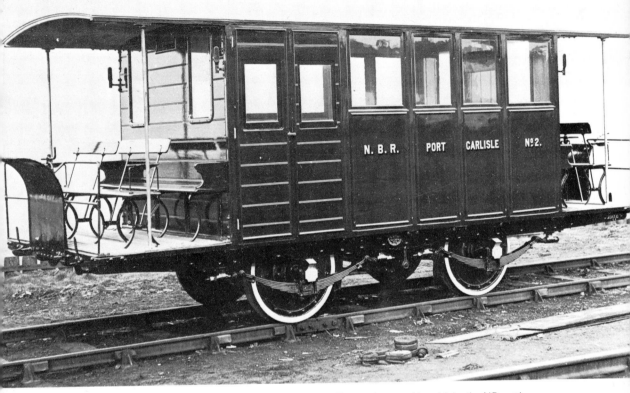

THE PORT CARLISLE BRANCH 'DANDYS'

The first of the famous 'Dandy' coaches on the Drumburgh and Port Carlisle Branch was built c1856 by a coachbuilder in Carlisle. It was attached to the rear of a conventional train and detached at Drumburgh where it was horse hauled over the line to Port Carlisle. It id not have a very long life and was replaced c1863 by the more famous No 1.

Above left: No 1 was to survive in service until the line was altered to be operated by steam traction from April 6th, 1914. It was then sold to become a pavilion at a local recreation club where it languished, undistinguished until called for to attend the Darlington centenary celebration in 1925, when it was returned to NB livery. Afterwards, it was placed on a plinth at Waverley Station, Edinburgh, until the advent of the 1939 war when it was removed to a place of safety. It was later placed on a plinth, at Carlisle Citadel station, where it remained until removed to form part of the Railway Museum at York./*BR*

Left: To supplement this vehicle, the NB put in service a more orthodox vehicle in the form of Composite No 24, but it appears that this car did not have a lengthy stay, although this is somewhat difficult to specify in that it never received the status of a 'Horse Carriage' in reports, being numbered in the locomotive hauled series./*LPC*

Above: In 1908, however, a second 'Horse Carriage' was built at Cowlairs and this took its place beside No 1 on the Branch, and was to last until 1914. Originally designed as a 'Toastrack' type of vehicle, this was later ammended by the closing of the passenger saloon. Unlike the other two vehicles, this was a one class only coach, although in some fairness, the 2nd class designation on No 1 became obsolete in 1891 when the North British Railway discontinued this classification./*A. Maclean Collection*

FREIGHT STOCK

The very simple lines early constructional practices are evident in this illustration of an Edinburgh & Glasgow low sided wagon, photographed c1860./*A. Maclean Collection*

No 21261 depicts another stage in the evolution of the open wagon with the large single wooden brake blocks operating on one wheel, wooden solebars and dumb buffers. All relevant data to the operator is on the solebar, the sides remaining blank./*Mitchell Library*

No 31735 was one of the last freight vehicles built for the North British. A Hurst Nelson product of 1922, the twin side doors opened outwards in place of the more customary drop downwards./*Motherwell Public Library*

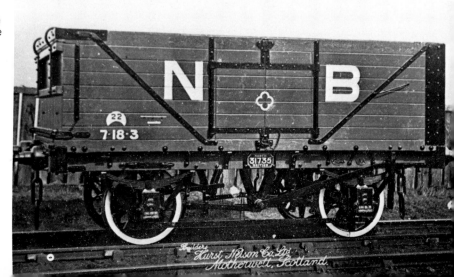

The Gunpowder Van was built by W. R. Renshaw & Co, of Glasgow in 1904. Painted vermilion, the shaded lettering was unusual for NB wagons. Normal door gear was not provided, the doors being secured by a mortice type lock operated by a key of 'padlock' type, copies of which were held at relevant points on the system. As LNER 765410, this vehicle was withdrawn in October 1946, but sister wagons lasted into the mid 1950s./ *A. Maclean Collection*

No 16230 was built in 1911 by Messrs Hurst Nelson & Co, of Motherwell. With a ten ton capacity, vans of this type were produced in large quantities a few lasting into the mid 1960s in revenue-earning use as apart from Departmental stock./ *Motherwell Public Libraries*

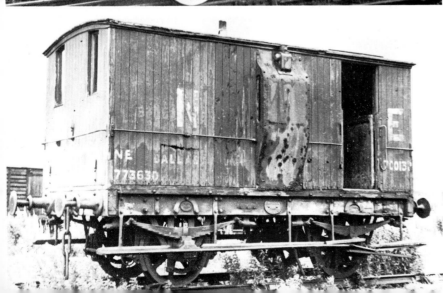

The NB goods brake van was of unique design. No 132 is seen here after being 'departmentalised' by the LNER. Built at Cowlairs in 1907, this vehicle is shown on her last resting place near Riccarton Junction./ *J. E. Hay Collection*

SPECIAL FREIGHT STOCK

Above: The creosote tank wagon, allocated to the Engineer's Department, carries all relevant data on the solebars. Brake blocks are of cast iron, and spring buffers are fitted, although grease remains the axlebox lubricant./*BR*

Below: The floor cloth wagon is a type which was unique to the North British. There were in fact two designs, both virtually identical, one of which is represented by No 25687 which had been built at Cowlairs in 1877. The wagon remained in service until May 1946./*BR*

Bottom: No 27322 must be somewhat unusual in that the floor was fitted inset into the frames, flush with the top of the solebar. Classified as a rail wagon, the carrying capacity was twenty tons. Although it is in NB livery, the shopping date on the solebar is May 1923, well into the LNER era./*BR*

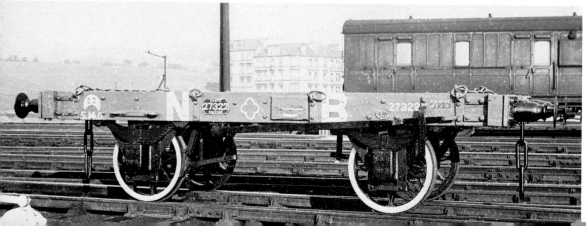

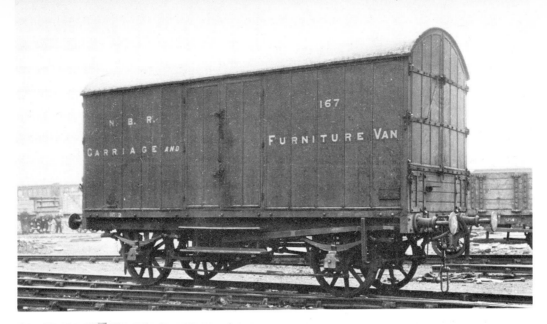

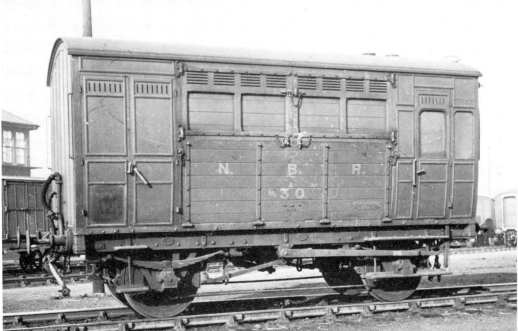

COACHING STOCK — NON PASSENGER

Top: Classified as coaching stock, but owing more to freight stock was this four wheel carriage & furniture van, No 167. Built at Cowlairs in 1893 as part of a small class of six, this vehicle survived, latterly as LNER 1036, until the late 1920's. Other of the class had a longer life, lasting until 1939/40 and even then lingering on as stores vans. */BR*

Above: One ubiquitous item of rolling stock in all fleets was the horse box, and this is represented by No 30. Built in 1912, it became LNER 1829, and lasted in traffic until June 1954, being broken up in the following year. This was the final design of NB horse box, construction taking place over the years from 1912 to 1921. */BR*

TAY BRIDGES

The first bridge over the Tay at Wormit was erected
to the designs of Thomas Bouch and publicly
opened in June 1878, although trains had crossed for
some months beforehand. This single track structure
fell with tragic loss of life during a storm on
December 28th, 1879, but had so proved its value
that a second bridge was erected, avoiding the
design errors of its predecessor and opened on June
20th, 1887.

Right: The first bridge during construction, taken
from the south bank of the Tay./*Dundee Public
Libraries*

Far right: Looking through the High Girders of the
first bridge towards Dundee./*Dundee Public
Libraries*

Below: The superstructure of Pier 42 of the new
bridge being erected by waterborne crane,
November 1885./*Dundee Public Libraries*

Below right: The testing of the new bridge was
carried out by six locomotives, operating in two
parallel groups of three. The operation is seen here
from the Esplanade on the north bank of the River./
Dundee Public Libraries

FORTH BRIDGES

The present Forth Bridge is the second to be built on the site, although it must be conceded that the first bridge got no further than a solitary pier. The latter succumbed to the aftermath of the Victorian discrediting of its designer, Sir Thomas Bouch.
Above: The pier of the first bridge is seen adjacent to the centre span of the second bridge, surmounted by a navigational light./*H. Beaton*

Above right: The second bridge is depicted under construction, a view taken from the south bank of the Firth./*St Andrews University Library (Valentines)*

BRIDGES

Right: Typical of the stone viaducts on the Edinburgh & Glasgow main lines is this specimen near Linlithgow. Designed by Robert Telford and built in 1839, the stonework has required some additional bracing over the years, but still plays an important part in the present day rail network./*BR*

Far right: This impressive viaduct at Glenfinnan, at the head of Loch Shiel, is on the Mallaig extension of the West Highland Railway./*A. A. Cameron*

FORTH BRIDGE FROM S. 10674 J.V.

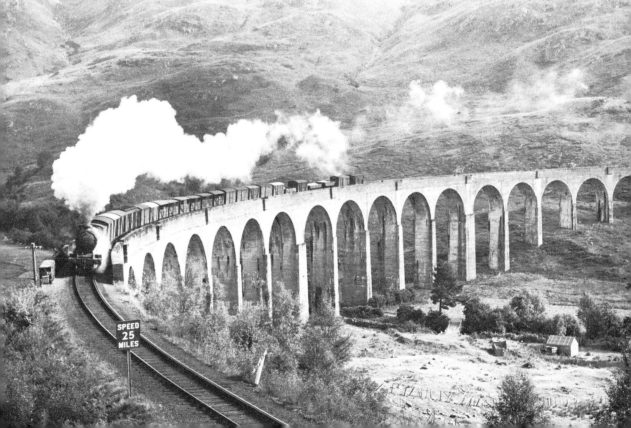

BERWICK ENGINE SHED

Above: The old roundhouse which afforded the North British engines accommodation at the southern end of the original main line is depicted here in this view dating from the first decade of the 20th Century. Plans for a new shed were drawn up during World War 1, but these were shelved and after the Grouping of 1923, motive power functions were transferred to the former North Eastern Railway Depot at Tweedmouth, over the River./*Scottish Record Office*

LADYBANK LOCO

Above right: 0-6-0 tender locomotive No 1365 poses with her crew and the Running Shed Foreman at Ladybank prior to the Grouping. Formerly No 271, the locomotive which dated from 1879 survived until July 1925, unrenumbered by the LNER. Note the massive shear legs for the adjacent road and the coaling stage in the background, both typical of North British practice./*Courtesy C. Meacher*

Right: The hand operated accident crane at the depot is virtually hidden by the staff, but clearly visible is the unusually shaped 'match' truck and brake van end. Of additional interest is the dumb buffers and side chains on the crane wagon./*Courtesy C. Meacher*

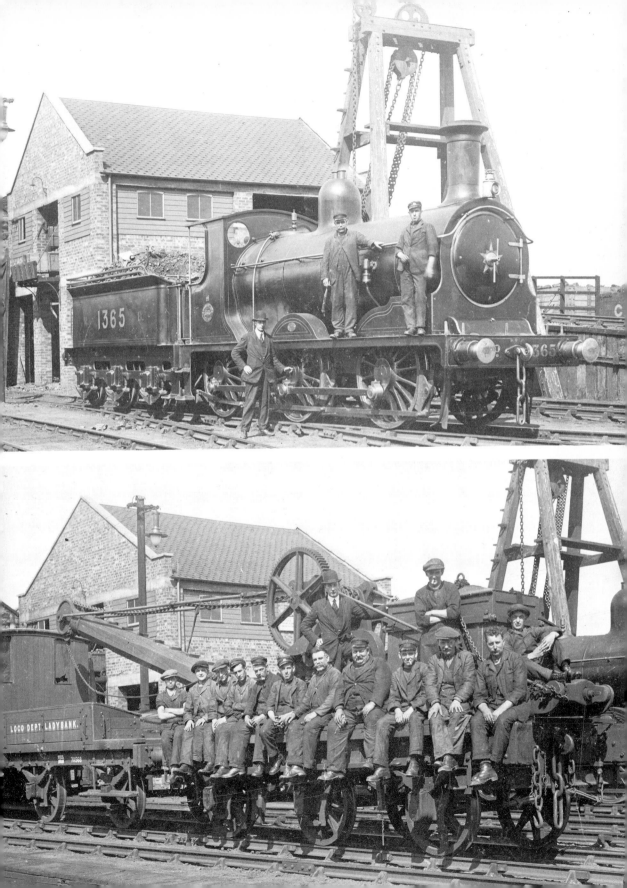

COWLAIRS SHED

Cowlairs locomotive Depot was built by the E&G Railway Company as an adjunct to their works. Accommodation was provided for 26 engines, and after closure, the building was absorbed by the expansion of the works. The shed frontage remained until the site was cleared completely after the Works closure. These views, by A. E. Lockyer, were taken in the late 1890's.

Top: Drummond 4-4-0T No 147, formerly named *Slamannan* is in the foreground. Behind this engine can be seen the three feather crest of the Prince of Wales, carried by Holmes 4-4-0 No 602 for the opening of the Forth Bridge in 1890.

Centre: The engine nearest the camera in the illustration is Drummond 0-6-0 No 583, later to become part of LNER Class J33. Facing this engine is Holmes 0-6-0 No 615. The engine in the centre is 4-4-0 No 578.

Bottom: An uncluttered view of the shed is taken from the down side of the main line.

EASTFIELD SHEDS

Opened in September 1904 to undertake the work of Cowlairs Shed which was then closed, the original engine shed at Eastfield shown here was destroyed by fire on Saturday June 28th, 1919. The shed was subsequently rebuilt and served the LNER and BR well. A further rebuild of the shed adapted it for the diesel age in the early 1970's, with the intention of making it the only engine shed for diesel locomotives in the Glasgow Area with full maintenance facilities.

Top: Shed interior, showing the large usage of wood in construction./*Scottish Record Office*

Centre: The old hand coaling stage./*Scottish Record Office*

Bottom: The steam breakdown crane with 4-4-0 locomotive 703./*Scottish Record Office*

COWLAIRS WORKSHOPS
Originally the workshops for the Edinburgh &
Glasgow Railway, the Cowlairs establishment was to
become the sole railway works building locomotives
and other rolling stock for the North British.

Above: The finishing shop, with a fine array of
motionwork./ *Scottish Record Office*

Below: The erecting shop./ *Scottish Record Office*

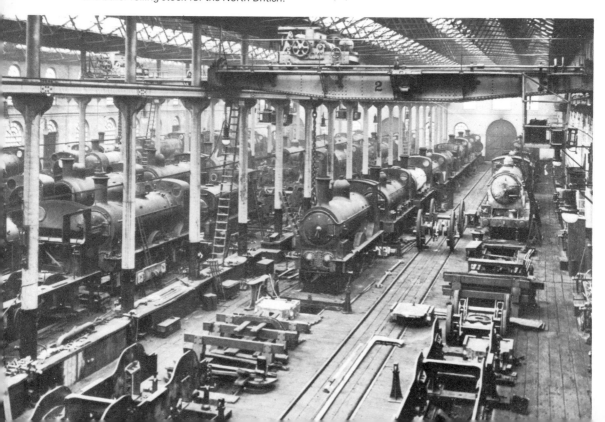

Top: The non-locomotive functions of the Works are illustrated here with a view of the carriage works with some of the fine Reid 9 compartment thirds under construction./*Scottish Record Office*

Above: A general view of the wagon shops with a row of twelve ton standard box vans awaiting to enter traffic./*Scottish Record Office*

COWLAIRS STATION

Left: This view of the station at Cowlairs before the platform was widened has the works on the left. In the down platform, Holmes 7ft 0in 4-4-0 No 603 has just arrived on an express. In the up platform are the brake trucks which will be attached to the front of the train in lieu of the locomotive for the descent into Queen Street Station. The clock tower of the old signal box at Cowlairs which was to be demolished in 1911 can be seen over the roof of the station buildings. The dual painting of the roofs of some of the carriages on the right in apparently grey and white is interesting as is the 'plug' cover for the oil lamp in position adjacent to the hole into which the lamp would be placed. Lamping was an operation requiring two men, one on the ground throwing up the lamp to the other on the roof of the coach./*LPC*

COWLAIRS INCLINE ROPE

Above: Two self explanatory illustrations relevant to the changing of the three-mile endless steel incline rope on the Cowlairs Incline in Glasgow. Both illustrations are from a commercially produced set of cards on the NB and date from the turn of the century./*J. Bryant Collection*

STATIONS

Below: The freight yard depicted is at Fort William on the West Highland Railway. The date is 1914./ *Locomotive & General Railway Photographs*

Bottom: The unusual platform canopy at Melrose, on the Edinburgh — Carlisle main line is well embellished by contemporary advertising./ *Scottish Record Office*

RURAL STATIONS

Above: Scotsgap Station, between Morpeth and Reedsmouth, was the junction for the Rothbury branch. The branch train is shown in the picture with 4-4-0T No 72 in charge. This engine, built in 1880, was the first of the class and in the Drummond tradition carried the name *Morpeth* for a time, although the town of that name was on the NER main line. In 1923, by then renumbered 1401, she was allocated to Blaydon (North Eastern Area) and was condemned in October 1924./*J. E. Hay Collection*

Below: Opened in 1894 was the charming wayside station of Corrour on the West Highland line. As was the case with most WH stations, it took the form of an island platform (right), and was connected to the loading bank (left) by the attractive wooden footbridge. The picture was one from a series on the line and is dated 1910./*J. Bryant Collection*

Corrour Station, Rannoch Moor

Macintyre's Series

SIGNAL BOXES

Above: Portobello East Signal Box was unusual for the NB in that it was located on a gantry. The cabin dated from September 26th, 1909, and controlled the junction where the 'Waverley' route to Carlisle and the East Coast Main Line diverge. It was near here that Robert Skelden was employed when he devised the basic principle of remote control of signals by mechanical means./*N. D. Mundy*

Left: Redding, on the Edinburgh & Glasgow main line, between Polmont and Falkirk, typifies the virtually 'standard' type of brick and timber construction as employed by the NB. The cabin was closed and demolished as part of rationalisation of signalling undertaken in connection with the Edinburgh & Glasgow line in early 1970./*A. Maclean*

Below: Thornton Station Signal Box, to the north of the former station proper, is of all wooden construction. Opened on July 3rd, 1910, the cabin is sited in an area which is prone to colliery working subsidences. The illustration was taken on April 9th, 1971, and the cabin is still operational although the station itself has been demolished./*N. D. Mundy*

Above: Invertiel Junction, one mile to the south of Kirkcaldy, controlled the point of divergence of the goods line to Auchtertool from the Edinburgh and Aberdeen Main Line. Of all brick construction, the box was opened on March 3rd, 1896, and survived as a block post until November 17th, 1963, when the box was closed and demolished. A new box, named Seafield was erected nearby to cater for the new colliery of that name./*A. Maclean*

Below: St Margarets cabin was an attractive box in an unattractive site. It controlled the main exit

from the shed and the East Coast Main Line in the vicinity. The box would appear to be an enlargement of an earlier building but the extension of the colour light signalling schemes and the elimination of the Motive Power Depot led to its closure./*A. Maclean*

Below: This small cabin, known as Cairntows, was merely an elevated ground frame with a cover. It controlled the exit from the St Leonards branch at Duddingston and the adjacent level crossing./*A. Maclean*

SIGNALS AND SIGNALLING

Above: This very early form of signal was located on the Port Carlisle Branch. Mounted on a wooden post, the control appears to be purely local./*R. Bryant Collection*

Above right: The early semaphore signals of the Company are represented by this view of a slotted post type. Note the lamp at the base of the post during the hours of daylight when the officers required their staff to wind down and extinguish the flame!/*M. Dagg Collection*

Below: The interior of a typical North British Railway signal box is depicted here by Morningside Road, on the Edinburgh Suburban line. On the North British, the signalman faced the traffic he was controlling. Signalman Forbes is in charge of the frame which was superseded in the 1960s under a resignalling scheme./*A. Maclean*

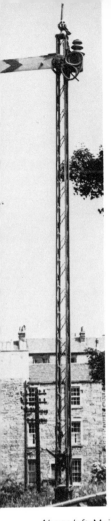

Above left: Main Line Distant signal at Trinity Station exemplifies the standard North British Railway lattice post signal. Note the absence of the signal ladder, the lamp being raised and lowered by a crank handle at the base of the post, operating a chain which passed up the centre of the lattice. The lamp descended a 'T' shaped iron bar on one side of the lattice.

Above centre: Bathgate Lower Station had a footbridge which restricted the sighting of the stop signal and in consequence a repeater arm was provided on the same post. The small bracket carries a standard North British shunt signal.

Above: Located at the exit from the largest locomotive depot in the NB was this small subsidiary arm which was controlled by St Margarets signal box./*A. Maclean*

Left: Situated between a tunnel mouth and a junction in a cutting, the only logical type of signal which could be provided was of the 'hanging home' variety. Trinity Junction Signal Box can be seen in the background and marks the location. The line going straight ahead was to Scotland Street Goods Station on the formation of the old Edinburgh, Leith and Granton Railway.

JUNCTIONS

Border Counties Junction, where the single track of the NB to Riccarton and Hawick diverged to the right from the NER Newcastle and Carlisle route. By the exercise of 'Running Powers' the NB could enter Newcastle Central from the west, but the North Eastern kept very strict control of passenger traffic on the intermediate stations between Hexham and the Tyneside stations served by the NB trains./*J. E. Hay Collection*

Bonnington, in the Edinburgh suburbs was the location where the former Edinburgh Leith and Granton Railway route from Scotland Street to North Leith crossed the later North British route from Edinburgh via Abbeyhill to Granton at right angles, on the level. In the illustration, J36 0-6-0 locomotive No 65334 stands on the crossing on August 4th, 1959. Initially reduced to single track, the junction was later totally removed./*W. S. Sellar*

Spean Bridge station, where the Highland Railway's Invergarry & Fort Augustus line left the West Highland line. This 1914 view shows the up platform, the nearest station nameboard merely indicating the name of the smaller line. The down platform is behind the photographer./*L&GRP*

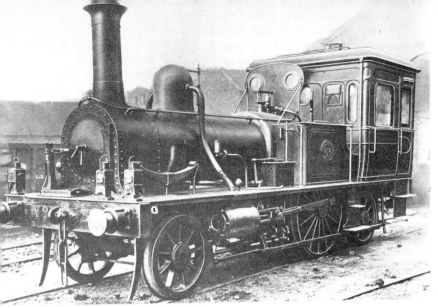

'FOR INSPECTION PURPOSES'

No 312A depicted here is perhaps the most celebrated of the older North British Railway locomotives. Her career was to span some 61 years, during which period she was to carry seven different numbers and sport the liveries of three owners. Built in 1850 by Neilsons of Glasgow, the Inspection Saloon was added in 1868, conforming to the coaching stock pattern of the period. The machine was disposed of by the NB in 1911./*Mitchell Library*

The equipment attached to the front bufferbeam of 4-4-0 No 693 was used by both engineering and operating departments, although it was more customarily used by the former. The locomotive was one of the class introduced in 1894 to Holmes design for work on the then new West Highland Railway. With the exception of one, which had been heavily rebuilt by Reid, all had been withdrawn by the end of 1924./*LPC*

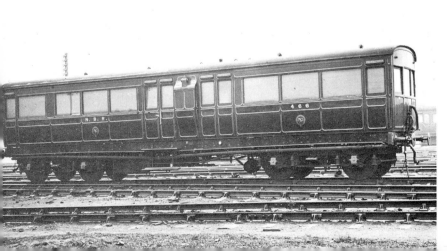

Saloon No 466 was one of a series of brake composites built in 1895 for the Edinburgh & Fort William through services. Rebuilt to the state depicted in 1918, it was to survive until July 1960, outlasting its sister vehicles by some 21 years./*BR*

2-4-0 PASSENGER

Above: Acquired from the Forth & Clyde Junction Railway in 1871, No 404 heads a short train of four standard North British coaches and six Incline Brake trucks up the Cowlairs Incline and away from Glasgow. The engine is shown as rebuilt by Wheatley in 1874 with small four wheel tender and other features of this notable engineer. The picture dates from c1890./*LPC*

0-6-0s

Above right: Double framed 0-6-0ST No 1069 originated from the Glasgow Works of Dubs & Co, in 1867. Originally numbered 209, she was one of three

similar machines, the original design for which was prepared with work on the Ballochney Incline on the Monkland Railway in mind. Fitted with a large round cab in 1893 and rebuilt in 1896, 1069 was withdrawn in 1920 and was sold out of stock two years later./ *Author's Collection*

Right: No 503 was one of a small stud of the Glasgow Bothwell and Hamilton Railway locomotives taken over by the NB in 1878. Built in the previous year, she survived, latterly as No 1373, until 1921 spending much of her life on Monkland Railway metals./*LPC*

WHEATLEY GOODS

The first Wheatley products from Cowlairs were two small 0-4-0 tender engines which emerged in 1868. *Below:* No 811 (formerly 358) is shown in virtually the original condition and presents a contrast with the rebuilt condition as portrayed *(Bottom)* by sister engine 1010, (old 357 & 810). 811 was the only 0-4-0 tender engine in the stock of the LNER, from whom it received the classification of Y10./*Photomatic Ltd and Author's Collection*

WHEATLEY PASSENGER

Above: Locomotive production under the Superintendency of Thomas Wheatley was geared towards freight engines, only a relatively small number of passenger machines being constructed. No 427 was one of the largest class of tender engine design and was built at Cowlairs in 1873. Rebuilt by Homes into the condition illustrated in 1890, she was not to be later rebuilt by Reid and was withdrawn during 1918. The Reid rebuilds were classified 'E7' by the LNER./*P. M. Westwater Collection*

Below: No 226, built at Cowlairs was   of the passenger tanks. Subsequently releg   to shunting work and renumbered 1172 in 1912, its life span extended from 1870 to 1920./*LPC*

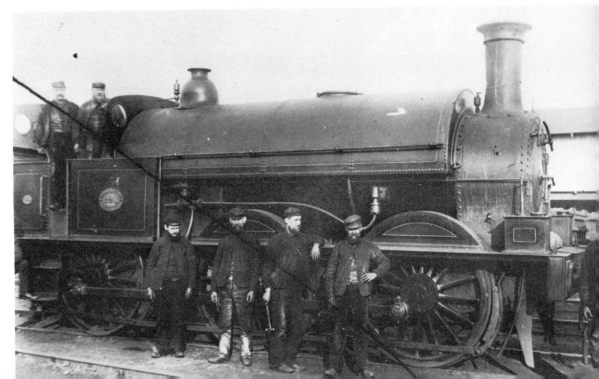

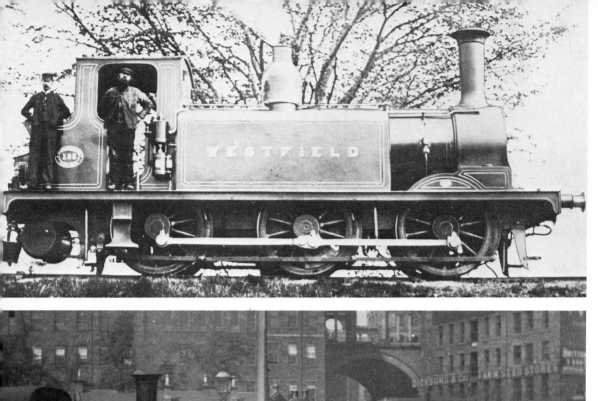

TERRIERS

Bearing a strong resemblance to the products of Brighton, these engines were larger. In accordance with Drummond practice, all carried names associated with their operational districts, although these were removed by Holmes after a comparatively short duration. Most were in service in 1923, and were classified 'J82' by the LNER

Top left: In Drummond livery is No 123 *Westfield*. This engine became No 1328 in 1918 and survived until 1926./*Author's Collection*

Centre left: The Holmes era of the 1890s is illustrated by No 297 at Waverley. Originally named *Penicuik* and later *Leith,* it became 1306 in 1918 and was withdrawn in 1925./*LPC*

Bottom left: No 49 depicting underframe detail. Built in 1878, it also carried two names in its career, these being *Sunnyside* and *Gretna.* Renumbered 1351 in 1919, it was withdrawn in 1924./*Real Photographs*

CLASS R 4-4-0Ts

Below: Built in 1883 at Cowlairs, No 268 *Bothwell* was the final Drummond 4-4-0T. As in the case of the 'Terriers', they were named to accord with their working areas, but the names were later removed. Subsequently renumbered 1465, it became LNER Class D51 No 10465 and as such survived until July 1928./*L. Ward Collection*

Bottom: Confusion indeed for the period locospotter, with the double numbering of this engine, shown below. Both numbers are correct, however, as the plate on the bunker depicts the duplicate list digits acquired in 1922. Originally named *Clydebank,* the engine was to remain in service, latterly as LNER 10461, until October 1932. From 1927, it worked trains on the former Great North of Scotland lines./*Author's Collection*

DRUMMOND SINGLE

In 1876, Messrs Neilson & Company of Glasgow put in hand the construction of two express locomotives for use on the Edinburgh & Glasgow main line. These two machines represented Dugald Drummond's first passenger design and it is claimed that they bear a strong resemblance to the 'Grosvenors' of the LBSCR, his former employers when he was assistant to Stroudley. These engines were never rebuilt and survived, latterly nameless until 1910. Illustrated is No 475, *Berwick,* its sister engine being No 474, *Glasgow.*/ *Mitchell Library*

DRUMMOND GOODS

No. 500 emerged from the Dubs & Coy works in Glasgow during 1879, one of a small batch of five contractor built locos to this basic design. The other 98 in the class were built at Cowlairs and differed in wheelbase. The engine is shown 'ex works' in original condition, and displays the dome safety valves which were altered after a boiler explosion to one of the class in 1882. Renumbered 1396 in 1920, the engine was to last until January 1923 when it nominally formed part of LNER Class J34, although not renumbered in the LNE series./ *Mitchell Library*

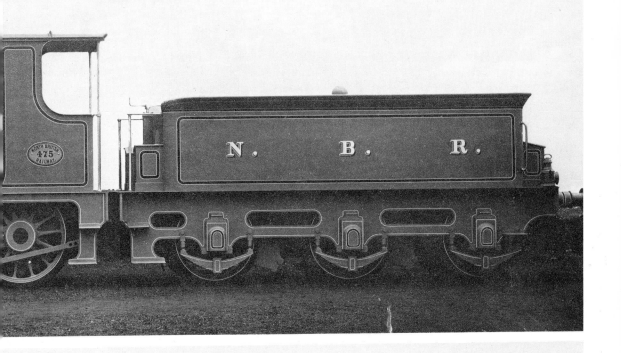

4-4-0 AT CITADEL

Below: With Caledonian Railway passenger stock forming the backcloth, Drummond Abbotsford class 4-4-0 No 488, formerly named *Galashiels,* awaits its next turn of duty in a centre road at Carlisle Citadel Station. Note the use of four of the six headlamp brackets, the discs forming the normal express passenger code, the lamps being in accordance with NB route practice. Photographed c1895, the locomotive was to be rebuilt in 1902 and renumbered into the Duplicate List in 1919 as 1362, two and a half years before being withdrawn./*A. Maclean Collection*

'CARLISLE'

Leaving the main Caledonian Railway line by which it achieved access to the Citadel Station at Carlisle, these three North British trains regain their own metals.

Top right: 4-4-0 No 36, built in 1890 to Holmes design and rebuilt as depicted in late 1918, heads a train of non corridor stock to Silloth, some 22 miles distant over what is often referred to as the only line in England operated by a Scottish Railway./*Real Photographs*

Centre right: Another 4-4-0, this time No 894 built in November 1909 heads northwards over the Waverley Route with a short train of Midland & North British Joint Stock. The locomotive was later in its career to be renumbered as 9894 and 2459 and survived as British Railways 62459 until September 1951. The carriages were also liable to come into LNER stock after 1928, and a number of Midland designs survived until the early 1950s, under LNER colours./*Real Photographs*

Bottom right: A typical train of Midland outline stock, with a twelve wheel dining car in the centre, is headed off the Waverley Route by Atlantic locomotive No 878 *Hazeldean.* The leading vehicle is a standard North British Railway nine compartment non corridor third./*Real Photographs*

NEWCASTLETON

Right: Newcastleton Station, locally known as Copshaw, forms the scene for the departure of this local train in the early days of the war. The intense activity on the platform is explained by the fact that the train conveyed Army volunteers from the locality./*M. Dagg*

WAVERLEY ROUTE

Far top: Intermediate class 4-4-0 locomotive No 331 (LNER 9331 and 2460) heads the 2.30 pm train from Edinburgh Waverley to Carlisle near Stobs Camp in 1919. The train is a mixture of rolling stock, with two six wheel thirds leading three more modern corridor vehicles. A bogie lavatory third and some vans bring up the rear./*R. B. Haddon*

Far centre: A six coupled locomotive, No 1082 of Wheatley design and Neilson build, vintage 1868, nears Stobs Camp Station on a Hawick to Newcastle train in 1920. The locomotive was to survive for a further five years, but never acquired LNER livery./*R. B. Haddon*

Far bottom: A Hawick to Carlisle Saturdays Only train near Stobs Camp, hauled by a six coupled locomotive of Class 'B' (LNER Class J35). The train is composed of predominently four wheel stock, the year is 1923./*R. B. Haddon*

HAWICK

Above: A view of the platforms taken during the first decade of the present century, with 2-2-2 locomotive No 1006 and train at the up platform. Originally built for the Edinburgh & Glasgow Railway by Beyer Peacock in 1856, it was to undergo several modifications during rebuilds before attaining its final form. Originally No 85, *Dullatur*, it was subsequently renumbered 43, 216, 806, and 1006 before being withdrawn in 1912./*R. B. Haddon Collection*

Below: A northbound train with Midland Railway type stock leading pauses for station duties in the down platform, while a mixed train of goods and passenger stock occupies the up line. Additional interest is provided by the small passenger set in the dock platform, comprising of third, first, third and brake four wheel stock./*P. M. Westwater Collection*

EAST COAST EXPRESS

Right: The North British was one of the few — if not the only main line railway company which had some principal passenger trains operated by the locomotives of another railway. Here, a North Eastern 4-4-0 of Class F1 (LNER Class D22) No 1537 exercises its running powers on a southbound express of six wheel stock to East Coast Joint Stock contour (NER Brake Third leading) past Dunbar West Signal Box about 1892. The North British was to challenge the North Eastern in the late 1890s and for a time 'frontiered' at Berwick-on-Tweed, but the NER was to gain a legal decision and resumed working to and from Edinburgh./*Scottish Record Office*

WAVERLEY FOUR COUPLED

Above: At the east end of the station, a former Edinburgh & Glasgow Railway 2-4-0 No 354 backs down on to its train. Built in 1862 as E&G 104 to the designs of W. S. Brown, she was rebuilt by Holmes In 1882 by which time she was NB 354. In 1909, her number was altered to 1012 in the 'duplicate' lists, and final withdrawal from traffic came in 1913./ *A. Maclean Collection.*

Below: At the western end, 0-4-4T No 475 pauses to replenish its water tanks after having worked a train into the capital. Under the rebuilding scheme for Waverley, platform numbers were displayed at the 'railway' end for the guidance of traincrews and one of these signs is adjacent to the locomotive. No 475 was built by the NB Locomotive Co, at Springburn in 1909, and as LNER 9475 was withdrawn in 1940 as the last North British engine of that wheel arrangement in service./ *D. Martin Collection*

WEST OF WAVERLEY

Below: A Reid Atlantic leaves the Mound Tunnel and runs through Princes Street Gardens towards Haymarket shed./*Rixon Bucknall Collection*

Bottom: No 1387, a Cowlairs express locomotive of 1879 passes the engine shed at Haymarket with a Corstorphine local train of then modern Reid bogie vehicles. Renumbered, 10387 was to be withdrawn in 1926 as LNER Class D28, and was the last of the Drummond express locomotives to survive./*Real Photographs*

THE FORTH BRIDGE APPROACHES

No 1323 pauses at North Queensferry Station before passing on the Bridge with an Edinburgh local train. A Drummond design built by Neilson in 1877 as No 478, for a time in the Drummond era she carried the name *Melrose*. Rebuilt in 1902 as illustrated and renumbered 1323 in 1918, the engine survived the grouping, being withdrawn in 1924 as part of LNER Class D27./*R. D. Stephen*

Another local train, this time of vestibuled stock pauses at North Queensferry with Atlantic No 510 *The Lord Provost* in charge./*R. D. Stephen*

The other end of the Bridge is depicted in this commercial card of Dalmeny Station with a local train for Glasgow entering from the north./ *A. Waterfall Collection*

66

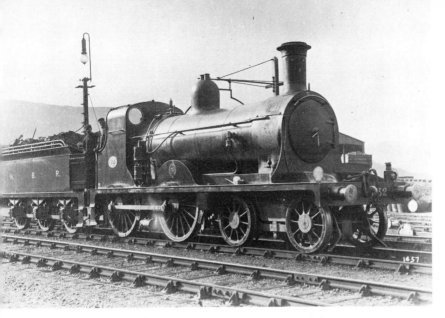

WEST HIGHLAND 4-4-0s

One of the class of locomotives designed for working the then newly opened West Highland Railway in 1894, No 232 pauses in the locomotive yard at Fort William. A none too successful design, with the exception of one locomotive which had been extensively rebuilt by Reid, the class suffered a relatively early demise. No 232 lasted until October 1921, latterly as duplicate list No 1437. Survivors at 1923 were classified D35 by the LNE, but none were to carry LNE numbers. /*LPC*

Prior to the outbreak of World War 1, an Intermediate Class 4-4-0 No 333 prepares to leave Morar with a Mallaig — Fort William train in 1914. /*L&GRP*

The Glen class 4-4-0 locomotives were to become synonomous with the West Highland. In this illustration, the first of the class, No 149 *Glenfinnan* makes a rare visitation to Fort William shed. This loco was allocated to Thornton Junction in Fife for most of its career. /*A. Maclean Collection*

DALMUIR PARK

Above: Former Drummond 4-4-0 No 487, a Neilson product of 1878, heads a local off the West Highland route towards Glasgow in 1906. The engine lasted in traffic until 1926, latterly as part of LNER Class D27, and with the NB duplicate list number 1361 which it attained in 1919./*W. A. C. Smith Collection*

Below: A 'West Highland Bogie' locomotive stands at the head of a local train of six wheeled carriages in the platforms at Dalmuir Park with a train for Glasgow (via Singer)./*W. A. C. Smith Collection*

POLMONT

Above: Former Wheatley 0-6-0 No 1139 (old 244) in the marshalling yard at Polmont in the final years of its career. Built in 1896 at Cowlairs, the engine was to be withdrawn in 1920, although some sister engines lasted until 1937, latterly as LNER Class J31. In the rear of the engine is guards brake van 38 and in the left background can be seen some of the extensive PO wagon fleet operated by Nimmo of Slamannan./*R. Honeyman*

Below: In contrast to 1139 is 433, here shown carrying the NB classification plate 'B' above the number plate. Built in 1916 at Cowlairs, the locomotive was still operating from Polmont when withdrawn in 1963. At the time of withdrawal the engine had been renumbered 64551 by BR, but still retained NB pattern lock-up safety valves./*R. Honeyman Collection*

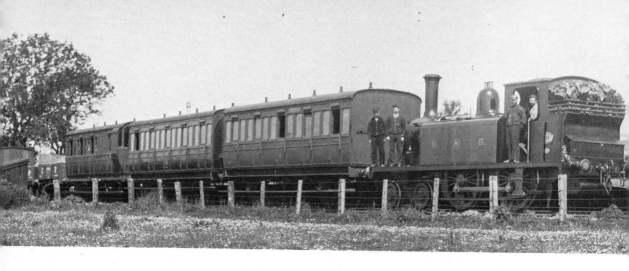

LOCAL PASSENGER AND FREIGHT

Top: A delightfully rural setting is brought to mind by this picture of a mixed passenger train, without first class accommodation, and with three freight vehicles bringing up the rear. Drummond 4-4-0 Tank locomotive No 110 provides the motive power, and every last square inch has been skillfully used in packing coal in the bunker. The locomotive, renumbered in 1920 as 1405, was withdrawn in December 1923./*LPC*

Above: Traversing the down slow line at Portobello with a local freight train is a Wheatley 0-6-0 No 1178, dating from 1871. Formerly No 126 before being placed on the duplicate list, this engine was to survive until August 1925, but was never renumbered by the LNER, although classified as J31 by them./*Rixon Bucknall Collection*

MAIN LINE TRAINS

Top: One of the few named trains on the North British was the 'Lothian Coast Express' which operated from Glasgow with through portions for watering places on the Firth of Forth. Both this train, and its partner the 'Fife Coast Express', were equipped with the latest type of coaching stock and handled by Scott class 4-4-0 locomotives. In the top illustration, No 359 *Dirk Hatteraick* suitably poses for the photographer with the set. Note the third vehicle in the set is one of the twelve wheel dining carriages which pre-dated the 'Craven's' of 1919.

Above: The North British Railway provided one ambulance train during World War 1 and as can be seen, the formation is basically made up of internally modified luggage vans, supplemented by two three compartment brake thirds and a twelve wheel dining carriage. All vehicles retain their NB livery with the addition of four white squares on the already maroon livery to form the 'red cross'. The locomotive is Scott class No 340 *Lady of Avenel./BR*

71

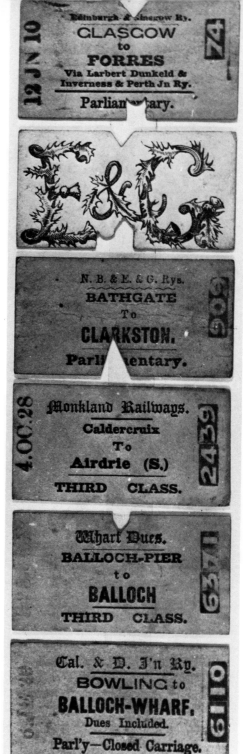

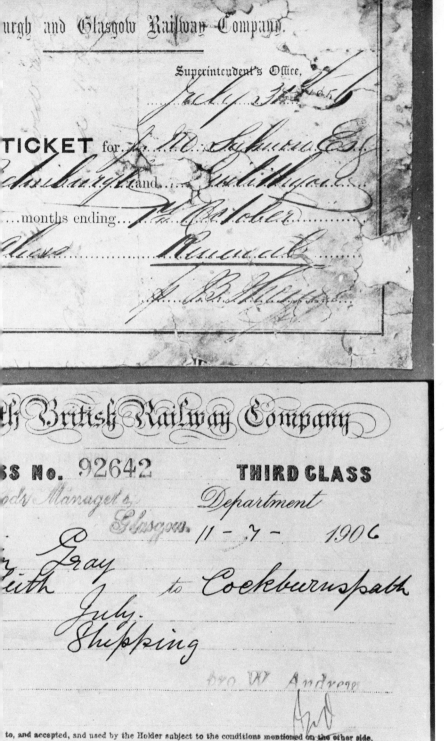

...urgh and Glasgow Railway Company.

Superintendent's Office,

July ... 1865

...TICKET for ... M. Sykes Esq.

...dinburgh and ... Linlithgow

...months ending ... 1st October

...lass ... Renewal

...

North British Railway Company

...ss No. 92642   THIRD CLASS

...ods Manager's   Department

Glasgow, 11 - 7 - 1906

... Gray

...eith   to Cockburnspath

July.

Shipping

pro W Andrew

...to, and accepted, and used by the Holder subject to the conditions mentioned on the other side,
AND IS NOT TRANSFERABLE.

TICKETS

Far left: The tickets illustrated here are from the year 1861, and feature six of the constituent lines of the North British. The tickets in the second row down are from the Edinburgh & Glasgow, the monogram being used on the reverse of tickets for stations off the parent system. Colours in the left hand column (reading down) are green, white, blue, white, yellow, and buff. In the right hand column, the top is buff, others pink. All are standard Edmonson card size./ *A. Maclean Collection*

Left: Both season ticket (of 1856) and free pass are paper tickets, issued from a pad./ A. Maclean Collection

ACCIDENTS

Above: This photo-montage needs no further caption, beyond mentioning that a train from Edinburgh at 3.55 am could hardly be the 'Flying Scotsman' as indicated./*R. Hollingworth Collection*

Right: Class 'B' 0-6-0 No 437 (LNER 1946 No 4555) comes to grief when it runs out of track at Bo'ness Low Junction and requires the help of the nearest steam crane./*R. Honeyman*

Above right: This Composite vehicle was the leading coach in the Glasgow — Edinburgh express which collided with a light engine at Ratho on July 3rd, 1917. It was to be rebuilt and survived, latterly as BR Sc32278E until condemned in December 1954./*Scottish Record Office*

RELICS

Above: The Slamannan Railway was opened to traffic in 1841, and to commemorate the event, a plaque was carved from stone and ultimately fitted to the base of a water tower at the foot of the Causewayend Incline near Manuel in Stirlingshire. On closure of the line and removal of the water tank, the plaque was despatched to Clapham Museum, but was severely damaged in the process. /*A. Maclean*

Left: When the Edinburgh & Glasgow Railway was opened in 1842, it ran from Dundas Street (later Queen Street), Glasgow to Haymarket, a distance of 46 miles. Mileposts of road pattern were erected, and more than half are still in use in 1974, notwithstanding the fact that the mileage was extended to 47¼ by the extension from Haymarket to Waverley Bridge in 1847. /*A. Maclean*

Right: Erected at the time of the reconstruction of the 1890s, the bronze statue of John Walker, the then General Manager overlooked the main booking hall at Edinburgh Waverley until removed to the Transport Museum in Glasgow when the booking hall was remodelled in 1970. The statue now fittingly reposes near the locomotive *Glen Douglas.* /*A. Maclean*

MISCELLANY

Above left: This cast plate, typical of many on the North British system, was located at the west end of Portobello Station Platform, and was always maintained in excellent condition. Unlike the alternative vitreous enamelled variety, the name of the Secretary is ommitted./*A. Maclean*

Left: The simple wooden structure which served as the tablet exchange platform, this example being at Kinniel, on the Bo'ness branch./*A. Maclean*

Above: A self-explanatory vitreous enamelled notice, in North British Railway style and colours of dark blue on white, which had partially succumbed to the weather. It was to be found at Crail Station, on the East of Fife line./*A. Maclean*

Above right: Reid Intermediate class 4-4-0 locomotive No 883 poses at Eastfield depot under a plethora of decorative bunting, prior to the working of a Royal Train./*C. L. Kerr Collection*

Right: Station staff at Dunfermline Lower Station in June 1896 get together for the camera. Included are the staff from the station bookstall!/*J. Emslie Collection*

FORTH FERRY

Above: An early camera captures the scene at Burntisland Pier before the advent of the Forth Railway Bridge. At the piers are a passenger paddle steamer and one of the famous train ferry steamers both of which operated to and from Granton and Burntisland. The original station is behind the two steamers. Only the facade still survives today as entry to the new station situated a little way up the hill./*Scottish Record Office*

Below: Famous for many years on the ferry service was the paddle steamer *William Muir*. Launched as No 37 from the yard of J. Kay & Sons at Kinghorn in 1879, she survived the withdrawal of most of the boats on the opening of the Forth Bridge in 1890. Rebuilt by Ramage & Fergusson of Leith in 1910, she lost her distinctive two funnels for the one illustrated. She made her last crossing on March 1st, 1937, from Burntisland, after which she was sold and broken up./*D. Young*

CLYDE STEAMERS

Above: Waverley was built in 1899 for the North British Steam Packet Company which came under Railway control in 1902. She was 'called up' during World War 1 and received an extension to the promenande deck, reaching forward to the bow. This feature was retained on her return to civilian duties. Mobilised again in Worl War II, she was lost during the Dunkirk evacuation. She is depicted here in NB colours in Loch Long during the summer of 1932./*D. Young*

Below: Marmion was the last vessel to be added to the North British Railway Clyde fleet, being built by A. & J. Inglis at Pointhouse in 1905. From 1915 to 1920 she operated under the Royal Navy, but is depicted here in more peaceful times departing from Craigendoran Pier in June 1931. With the advent of World War II she was again 'called up' and after surviving the Dunkirk evacuation, was bombed and sunk in shallow water at Harwich in 1941./*D. Young*

London & North Eastern Railway

NORTH BRITISH SIX COUPLED

Above: Holmes class 'D' 0-6-0 No 9249 rests outside the Kipps shed in 1937. This engine was one of two which replaced the smaller J31 class Wheatley engines which had been specially cut down to operate under a low bridge on the Gartverre Branch in Lanarkshire. In time, 9249 and its fellow J33 were replaced by cut down J36 engines./*C. Lawson Kerr*

Above right: An unmodified J36, formerly Holmes class 'C', reposed in the shed yard at the small shed at Fort William in June, 1927. Note the comparatively rare water column serving two roads, to the right of the engine./*H. C. Casserley*

Right: The largest freight locomotives on the North British were those introduced by Reid in 1914 and which became LNER J37s. In this illustration, one of the class, No 9073 draws away from the North Eastern railway station at Killingworth, to the north of Newcastle, with a southbound stock train, the leading vehicle of which was taken over by the LNER on the dissolution of the Midland & North British Joint Stock in 1928./*Photomatic Ltd*

BERWICK

Above: A former North Eastern Railway locomotive, LNER Class J21 No 152 of Tweedmouth shed, heads an Up local passenger train from the Eyemouth branch near Berwick in 1927. The leading two vehicles are sheeted fish wagons, followed by three NB coaches, two of which are four wheeled./*C. J. L. Romanes*

Above right: Signalled for the loop, a local freight train passes the same location with NBR Class 'B' 0-6-0, LNER No 9853, leading. Later in its career, the engine was to become 4465 in the LNER renumbering scheme./*C. J. L. Romanes*

Right: North of Berwick, near the station at Reston, a NB 0-6-0 No 274 helps out NE 4-6-2 No 2400 on an East Coast express in the innaugural year of the grouping, 1923./*LGRP*

SENTINEL RAILCARS

In an effort to reduce costs, the LNER introduced the steam railcars into Scottish Area Workings from the late 1920s. Although the cars were painted in a gay livery of green and cream, and carried the names of famous stagecoaches of the past, they were never the success which had been hoped for. The Scottish Area operated fourteen railcars and one trailer car, all the power units being obtained from Sentinel Cammell. There were several differing types within the broad classifications, and depicted here are two of them.

Top: No 312 *Retaliator* at Aberfoyle, in 1936./*C. Lawson Kerr*
Above: No 31 *Flower of Yarrow* 'on shed' at St Margarets. Although numbers and classifications were in the coaching stock series, they were stabled at Motive Power Depots, which did not assist in keeping them clean./*Real Photographs*

CASCADED CARRIAGES

After the Grouping of January 1923, the former North British Railway lines were allotted vehicles from other constituent lines made available by their displacement in turn by new building. In some instances, these old coaches provided an improvement in comfort over the native animal! All incomers were numbered within the North British series.

Above: From the Great Eastern Railway came this five compartment six wheel first. No 32165 was built at Stratford in 1891 as GE No 82, and like its NB fellows was fitted with the Westinghouse brake and incandescent gas lighting./*Courtesy W. T. Stubbs*

Below: A product from the dissolution of the Midland & North British Joint Stock in 1928 was this six wheel vestibuled brake van. Formerly M&NBJS No 166, 319 was built, not surprisingly, at Derby in 1899./*Courtesy W. T. Stubbs*

Bottom: A result of a straight purchase from the London Midland & Scottish Railway Company, this former Highland Railway bogie brake van came to the LNER (Southern Scottish Area) in 1944. Three former Caledonian Railway brakes were purchased simultaneously to work traffic from Glasgow to Perth and Dundee. All four were withdrawn by mid 1947./*BR*

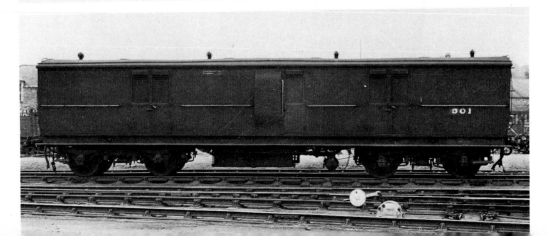

STRANGERS

Above: In April 1927, the LNER gave permission for the Reid Macleod steam turbine locomotive built by the North British Locomotive Company at Springburn to be track tested over the Glasgow and Edinburgh main line. Two vestibuled carriages were supplied from Southern Scottish Area stock. In the illustration, the special is shown on arrival at Edinburgh Waverley, adjacent to the wall mounted 'North Central Signal Box . This structure still survives as the Waverley Train announcer's box./ *Mitchell Library*

Below: A rare visitor to Edinburgh in the form of an Ivatt GNR Atlantic locomotive, No 4452, is captured by the camera while 'on shed' at Haymarket in July 1939./ *C. Lawson Kerr*

ADOPTED DESIGNS

Below: A development of the Great Central Railway Director class was the first new class of locomotive to enter top line service on the North British after the Grouping. In the true NB tradition they carried the names of characters from the works of Sir Walter Scott. The locomotive illustrated is No 6395 *Ellen Douglas,* which is coupled to the tender of 6396 at Ferryhill shed, Aberdeen on June 22nd, 1927./*H. C. Casserley*

Bottom: Although forming only a small proportion of the total in the class, the Gresley moguls of the K2 class 2-6-0 ultimately gravitated to the West Highland line operations, and most of the Scottish engines were to receive names of Lochs sited near the line. Most also were fitted with new side window cabs as seen in this illustration of No 4697 *Loch Quoich*, shunting at Crianlarich in 1937. Note the green and cream painted camping coach on the extreme right./*C. Lawson Kerr*

FOR EXHIBITION

Left: Reid Class 'H' Atlantic locomotive in the full North British livery but with the lettering of the London & North Eastern Railway on the tender, No 874 *Dunedin* was thus prepared for exhibition to the directorate of the new concern in London to assist in the selection of the new livery./*BR*

Below left: A sister engine, fitted with the Worthington Pump apparatus, by then renumbered 9903 on exhibition at Edinburgh Waverley in the company of the St Margarets Steam Breakdown Crane, 770517./*C. J. L. Romanes*

MORNING DEPARTURE

Below: The crew of London & North Eastern Railway Class A1 Pacific No 2566 (later 67) *Ladas* put the final touches to the grooming of their steed before leaving Edinburgh Waverley on the Up 'Flying Scotsman' for London (Kings Cross). A sleeping car of ECJS origin lies in an adjoining road./*BR*

4-4-0s

Top: Scott class 4-4-0 (LNER D29) No 9900 *The Fair Maid* leaves the City of Perth with a train for Edinburgh in the early years of the Grouping. As Perth General was classified an 'open' station, tickets were collected at the platform on the left before incoming trains ran forward into the terminal. / *Real Photographs* .

Above: Glen class 4-4-0 No 9291 *Glen Quoich* hauls a train of predominently LNER vehicles on a working to the Fife Coast resort of Crail past the Inverkeithing East Distant signal.

STOBS CAMP

Top: A Sunday Excursion from Edinburgh to Silloth passes the station at Stobs Camp during the summer of 1928 headed by Intermediate (D32) 4-4-0 No 9886 piloting a Scott class 4-4-0, both resplendent in the LNER green livery./*R. B. Haddon*

Above: In the following year, on more mundane duties, Class D30 No 9426 *Norna* heads a rake of non vestibuled vehicles on a Carlisle to Edinburgh local near Stobs Camp./*R. B. Haddon*

REID ATLANTICS

Top: No 9879 *Abbotsford* heads an afternoon express from Carlisle past the carriage sidings at Craigentinny, near Edinburgh in 1926./ *Author's Collection*

Centre: Former GNSR 4-4-0 acts as pilot engine to the 4-4-2 No 9876 *Waverley* on the afternoon fish train for London at Aberdeen in 1935. The pilot is marshalled inside the train engine in accordance with standard NB practice, and will be detached at Dundee./ *P. J. Symes Collection*

Bottom: Ten years later and nearing the end of its career, 9879 *Abbotsford* heads the 4.10pm Edinburgh — Perth past Haymarket Sheds. The Pullman car, second from the engine was one of five third class vehicles allocated to the Scottish Area domestic services before World War II./ *C. Lawson Kerr*

REID TANKS

Top: In 1904, W. P. Reid introduced to the North British Railway a light tank design with a six coupled wheelbase and outside cylinders. Classified as 'F' on the NB, they became J88 on the LNER. Illustrated is No 8347 'on shed' at Eastfield in the company of the black liveried A4 No 4462 *William Whitelaw* in May 1946.

Centre: In 1909, two tank designs originated, a passenger tank with the 0-4-4 wheel arrangement illustrated by No 9356 at Stirling in September 1937, and a mixed traffic tank of the 0-6-2 type, batches of which were to be built until 1924.

Bottom: No 9166, a NB Locomotive Company product of 1916, stands in the Cowlairs station loop in the mid 1930s, equipped with all the accoutrements of the 'Incline Pilots', and against a backcloth of grey Springburn tenements./*P. J. Symes Collection*

OUT OF SERVICE

Top left: When new in 1881 this North British Railway locomotive carried the name *Anstruther* and served that community. In 1930, her days numbered and her identity almost obscured by dirt and decay, as LNER 10426 she lies forlornly surrounded by a stockade of sleepers, only her boiler active as steam is led from her tubes into a shore installation. Yet an air of dignity still is present on this lowly task./ *A. Maclean Collection*

Centre left: In the yard at Cowlairs, another North British engine lies, but this one will be restored to traffic for almost a further decade. No 10180 of the J31 class awaits attention to her boiler before returning,to traffic on services which will include the Gartverrie Branch in Lanarkshire for which task the boiler mountings were reduced to take account of the very severe headroom provided under one bridge./ *A. Maclean Collection*

Bottom left: In a similar state of undress is D49 Shire class 4-4-0 No 310, *Kinross-shire,* although this engine is dignified by being in the full LNER green livery./ *H. C. Casserley*

'SOUTH QUEENSFERRY GOODS'

Below: Former North British Railway 0-6-0 No 9058 (later 4517) awaits the signal ro propel her brake van on to the main line at Dalmeny Junction from the branch line from Port Edgar, near South Queensferry. At one time a main line, the branch lost much of its importance (and its traffic) when the Forth Bridge was opened in 1890. In the same year, the closure of the passenger station at Port Edgar took place./ *Author's Collection*

NORTH EASTERN ENGINES

Top left: Before the impetus of the Gresley Pacific locomotives, North Eastern Railway locomotives handled the crack East Coast expresses southwards from Edinburgh. Here, C7 4-4-2 No 716 and D20 4-4-0 No 2107 leave Edinburgh with a southbound express./*BR*

Centre left: The Berwickshire Railway station at Duns provides the setting for this illustration of Class D17 4-4-0 No 1621, seen here in 1927 at the head of two venerable North British Railway six wheelers./ *C. J. L. Romanes*

Bottom left: North Eastern freight locomotives of the J24 class were allocated for some time to sheds on the former North British Area. No 5603 (1946 numbering) is seen here at Galashiels acting as yard pilot soon after its arrival north of the border, one of the last to come north./*C. Lawson Kerr*

CRIANLARICH

Above: Class K4 2-6-0 No 3444 *Lord of the Isles* draws away from the station at Crianlarich on the 3.49pm train to Glasgow (Queen Street) during July 1939./*C. Lawson Kerr*

MIKADO

Built to the design specification of Mr. Nigel Gresley, these magnificent machines were put to work on the steeply graded and tortuously curved Edinburgh and Aberdeen main line.

Above left: No 2005 *Thane of Fife,* the only one of its type to be equipped with a single chimney passes a typically Caledonian Railway signal near Stonehaven in July 1938.

Left: The conditions of wartime had been experienced for almost four years as No 2006 *Wolf of Badenoch* heads a northbound express near Stonehaven in July 1943. This engine was rebuilt as a Pacific in May of the following year, but it is claimed that the performance of the rebuilt machines

was not up to the performance of the original. Note the white flashes behind the front buffers, presumably to aid visibility in the 'blackout'./
C. Lawson Kerr

GREEN A4

Above: No 4484 *Falcon,* one of eight locomotives of the A4 type to appear in lined green livery, heads the 'Flying Scotsman' near Grantshouse in 1937. Placed in traffic in February 1937, and allocated to Haymarket shed, this engine was repainted in the standard 'garter blue' livery before the end of that year. Included within the formation can be seen one of the famous triplet dining car sets of 1924./*E. R. Wethersett*

WARTIME ERA

Above: Two Glens, Nos 9242 *Glen Mamie* and 9258 *Glen Roy* (later 2482 and 2470 respectively) double head a special passenger train near Finnart above Loch Fyne, in September 1941. During the war, some of the West Highland was a prohibited area for civilians, and the regular passenger services were severely curtailed, due to the naval and military functions along its length./*C. Lawson Kerr*

Below: The Class V4 light 2-6-2 was the last locomotive design to be produced under the jurisdiction of Sir Nigel Gresley before his untimely death in 1941. Reported as being the possible precursors of a standard class, only two were in the event constructed, both machines settling in former North British territory. The small boiler fitted to these engines is evident in this illustration of the first of the class, No 1700 *Bantam Cock,* seen at the head of a westbound local from Edinburgh in August 1947./*C. Lawson Kerr*

Above: During the war, work was carried out to rebuild locomotives of the former Great Central 0-8-0 type into heavy shunting tank locomotives with the intention of forming a standard class. Only thirteen were actually rebuilt, and one of the two allocated to Scotland, No 9925, is shown 'on shed' at Eastfield in 1947. Note the cast totem on the bunker which was carried through the British Railways era until withdrawal./*C. Lawson Kerr*

Below: The dark days of World War II are evoked by this illustration of the entry to Queen Street Station in Glasgow on December 16th, 1943. This part of the station was built in 1842 and it was to survive virtually intact until the reconstruction work of the late 1960s when all traces were removed. The building on the right was the former E&G headquarters, itself rebuilt from a church, and known over the system by the name of a former clerical incumbent, the Rev Wardlaw, as the 'Wardlaw Kirk'.

BURNMOUTH PACIFICS

Left: Class A3 4-6-2 No 2750 *Papyrus* in much begrimed state passes near Burnmouth with the down 'Junior Scotsman'. Although lacking the glamour of the parent train, the operational difficulties were if anything larger with a larger number of through portions being carried. Note that the second vehicle from the engine is fitted with a luggage compartment without brake equipment./*E. R. Wethersett*

Below: The post-war version, 'Flying Scotsman' set is in the charge of A3 class No 65 *Knight of Thistle*. Although the main part of the rake is of the all steel construction, the dining portion is still composed of wooden bodied vehicles, as is the rear brake./*E. R. Wethersett*

FOUR WHEEL PUGS

Top right: The saddle tank locomotives, although credited to Matthew Holmes, had an origin many years earlier in a standard Neilson & Company product. Indeed, the first two were purchased from that firm. Most were only equipped to deal with basic shunting work, but one, shown here as the LNER No 8101 was vacuum fitted for coaching work in the Dunfermline Area. She is here 'on shed' at Eastfield in 1947, equipped with one of the small four wheel tenders with which a number of the class were fitted. The Vacuum control gear is shown *(centre)./ C. Lawson Kerr*

Below: Formerly numbered 9529, this little Sentinel 0-4-0 was the only engine not built to a North British design which was numbered in the NB series, (if one discounts the 4-6-2-2 No 10000). She is shown here in the livery and number of May 1945 at Hawick depot in October 1949. Note the typical North British shunter's step between the axleboxes. Built in 1927, she survived until January 1959, nearly all of that time being spent either at Hawick or Kelso./*Author's Collection*

COWLAIRS JUNCTION

Below: Sporting the post war number of 37, Class A3 Pacific *Hyperion* approaches the station in August 1947 with an express from Edinburgh. Note the one lever ground frame and the shunting signal with its open 'X' shaped arm./*E. R. Wethersett*

4-4-0

Bottom: Despite a rather forlorn appearance, this locomotive was to be overhauled to carry the full British Railways insignia, although its subsequent life was to be numbered in months, rather than years. Built in 1894 as No 732, it was to follow the progression through the normal links from top as newer machines were built, but had a long association with one main line depot, being at St Margarets until the outbreak of World War II. In the past war years, it was sent to aid the motive power situation on the old Great North of Scotland lines, and never returned to a North British depot./*E. R. Wethersett*

MOUND TUNNEL

Above: Class V2 2-6-2 locomotive No 844 emerges from the mouth of the tunnel into Princes Street Gardens with the 1.09pm local train to Dundee in March 1949, although both engine and leading vehicle are still in former Company livery. The engine headcode is misleading in that the train called at most intermediate stations en route./*C. Lawson Kerr*

Below: Bearing the original livery accorded to British Railways secondary passenger locomotives, No 62706, *Forfarshire* heads an Edinburgh to Dundee local out of the Mound Tunnel into the March sunshine in 1949. Coaching stock in the illustration still retains the LNE varnished teak livery, although the numbers are prefixed 'E' in the LNE shaded style./*C. Lawson Kerr*

British Railways

EAST COAST FLOODS
Above: Almost exactly 100 years after severely inclement weather had caused a 'washout' on the original North British, similar climate prevailed and numerous bridges on the East Coast main line were swept away. In this illustration, D49 class 4-4-0 No 62706 *Forfarshire* and A4 Pacific 60012 *Commonwealth of Australia,* both in the early British Railways livery, test the temporary structure which replaced bridges 137 and 138 on October 24th, 1948. The two vehicles behind the A4 are NB and MSLR saloons./*BR*

EARLY BRITISH RAILWAYS
Above right: Class 07 2-8-0 No 63038, one of 200 purchased by the LNER from the War Department, heads an up goods climbing to Falahill past Bowland in October 1949. This St Margarets locomotive was soon to receive the number 90038 in the British Railways numbering series, and was one of the few to carry a BR number in the LNER range.

Right: The Great Northern Railway 4-4-0 locomotives which were transferred to the lines of the North British after 1923 did not meet with a particularly fond welcome. No 62208 (old 3057) languishes at the rear of Eastfield Motive Power Depot in Glasgow awaiting the cutters torch after withdrawal from Hawick in July 1950. The smokebox handrail is worthy of note./*C. Lawson Kerr*

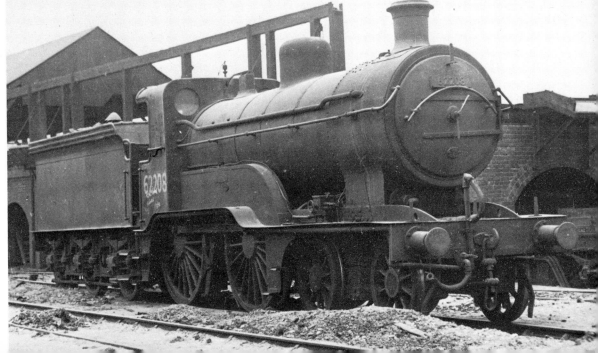

CAPITAL EVENING

Below: The clock on the North British Hotel approaches the starting time of the 5.39pm train to Corstorphine which is in the care of V1 2-6-2T loco No 7670. Flanking the train in this April 1948 photograph are B1 4-6-0 No 61245 *Murray of Elibank* (centre) and 2437 *Adam Woodcock* of the NB superheated Scott class (LNER D30). The leading vehicle on the local train is one of the standard nine compartment North British non corridor vehicles./*C. Lawson Kerr*

WAVERLEY APPROACHES

Right: Former NBR Class 'A' 0-6-2T locomotive No 907 as British Railways No 69144

leads a local freight train over the maze of trackwork at the Eastern end of Waverley Station in September 1959. The gradient on the line through the tunnels in the background is the steepest to be found on the East Coast Route between Edinburgh and London./ *W. J. V. Anderson*

Below right: Class A3 4-6-2 No 60098 *Spion Kop* of Haymarket Depot nears the Capital with the down 'Fair Maid' from London to Perth in June 1958. The main line metals at this point went through the centre of St Margarets Motive Power Depot./*C. Lawson Kerr*

'THE UP CAPITALS'

Above: Gresley A4 4-6-2 No 60029 *Woodcock* heads the up 9.45am train from Edinburgh non stop to London, on the ascent of Cockburnspath Bank in the summer of 1951. This train, which was subsequently renamed 'The Elizabethan' from 1953, achieved the distinction of being the longest non stop run in Great Britain after World War II. The advent of diesel power made the inclusion of a stop at Newcastle compulsory to change crews, and therefore this train can be said to have been steam's finest (post war) hour!/*E. Treacy*

GRESLEY SIX COUPLED

Top right: Built for service over former NB lines, the J38 class 0-6-0 was introduced in 1926 and a total of 35 were built. No 65918 is seen here breasting the

summit of the Edinburgh Outer Circle Suburban line at Morningside Road, with a Niddrie — Cadder freight in 1958./*A. Maclean*

Centre right: A development of the J38s, the J39 class was ultimately to total some 289 machines built between 1926 and 1941. In the illustration, No 64844 with NER tender, had just arrived at the Berwickshire station of ~~Reston~~ with its one coach (Brake Composite) from the port of Eyemouth./*D. Martin*
BURNMOUTH

Bottom right: J39 No 64975 barks its way past the Haymarket Motive Power Depot with a Corstorphine local train of mixed LMS and LNE vehicles in August 1959./*C. Lawson Kerr*

'YORKIES'

Built by the Yorkshire Engine Company between 1911 and 1913, the 30 machines which comprised NBR Class 'M' (LNER C15) remained virtually unaltered throughout their career.

Above: No 67455 (NB No 4) leaves Perth with a local train for Ladybank, via Newburgh, comprising of a full third (No 82100) and a brake composite, both to LNER designs. The locomotive spent many years at Perth before being transferred to Aberdeen in 1950 where it remained, often as station pilot, until withdrawn in 1955. The Perth — Ladybank passenger service was withdrawn from September 17th, 1955, although the line still deals with freight and passenger diversions. /*J. Robertson*

Below: One of the three locomotives specially fitted for working the Arrochar and Craigendoran 'push-pull' service. No 67474 was technically the last of the class, being condemned on April 12th, 1960 a few days after its partner on this service 67460. The two coaches were specially modified in 1940 and did not venture far afield. The train is depicted awaiting the signal at Arrochar to return to Craigendoran on March 21st, 1959. /*W. S. Sellar*

CLASS C16

Below: Former North British Railway Class 'L' 4-4-2T No 444, renumbered by British Railways 67488, leaves Polmont Station without headcode on the front of a short train of LMS carriages for Falkirk Grahamston and Larbert in March 1957. Built by the North British Locomotive Company, in 1916, she was to remain in service for over 43 years./*W. J. V. Anderson*

Bottom: A sister engine No 67492 (NBR 448) stands outside the two road engine shed at North Berwick, well groomed in readiness for a special train on August 26th, 1958. Although the branch from Drem had long been the preserve of Gresley 2-6-2T engines, for a short period in that year 67492 was the 'branch engine'. A St Margarets locomotive all her life, she was withdrawn in March 1960./*W. S. Sellar*

'THE BRANCH AND THE TWIG'

The branch line from St Boswells to Kelso was one of the oldest on the North British network. At the intermediate station of Roxburgh Junction, a branch line diverged to the town of Jedburgh.

Above: Class D30 4-4-0 locomotive No 62440 *Wandering Willie* awaits departure from Kelso Station on a local passenger train for St Boswells.

Below: After the withdrawal of the passenger train service, Class J37 0-6-0 No 64577 stands with a short freight train in the platform at Jedburgh before leaving for the junction. The overall roof had by this time been removed and the former locomotive depot handed over to the local road motor.

THE AULD LAUDER LIGHT

Opened for traffic on July 2nd, 1901, the branch from the Waverley Route at Fountainhall to the Royal Burgh of Lauder suffered operationally from a line speed restriction of 25mph and severe axle load restrictions. The latter was to prove troublesome after the demise of the small 4-4-0T locomotives in the early 1930s and although the passenger service was withdrawn on September 10th, 1932, freight traffic continued until October 1st, 1958. Two ex GER 0-6-0T locomotives, Nos 7329 and 7399 (later 8492 and 8511 respectively) were fitted with tenders to convey water, the tanks remaining empty to reduce weight.

Below: No 68511 leaves the main line junction and crosses the Gala Water by the single 50 ft span stone bridge.

Bottom: The purely functional design of the station buildings is depicted by those at Oxton, the only intermediate station. Note the wooden platform construction.

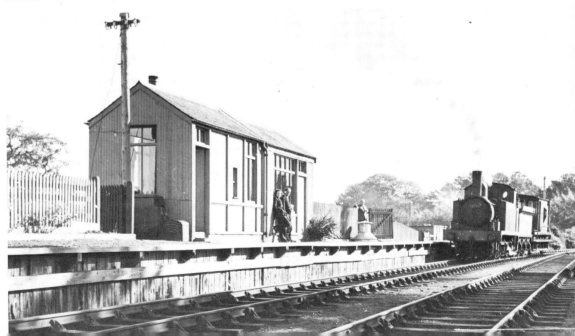

GALASHIELS AND PEEBLES

Above: A train from Edinburgh to Hawick stands in Galashiels Station in October 1949 headed by Class D30 4-4-0 No 62428 *The Talisman* in the early British Railways livery./*C. Lawson Kerr*

Below: Successor to the old NB engines, an LNER B1 4-6-0 No 61029 *Chamois* heads an Officers' Special train at Peebles East on March 14th, 1962, after the closure of the line./*D. Martin*

'INTERMEDIATES'

Below: NBR '882' class 4-4-0 No 884 is shown in later life as LNER D32 class No 2445 heading a local passenger train past Craigentinny Box near Edinburgh in the early days of nationalisation. The engine was not to carry a British Railways number, being withdrawn in 1949 after 43 years service./*J. Bryant Collection*

Bottom: Differing in details from the previous class, the LNER accorded the classification of D33 on the class of locomotive represented by No 62460, here seen passing Old Kilpatrick Station, on the western outskirts of Glasgow with a local freight train for Cadder Yard, in May 1951, three months before withdrawal./*C. Lawson Kerr*

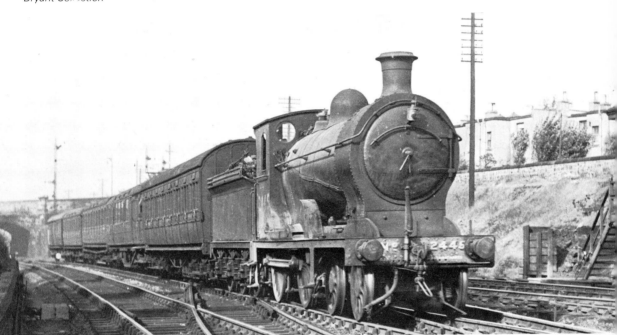

SUBURBAN PASSENGER

Above: Glen class 4-4-0 No 62487 *Glen Arklet* stands in the platform at Morningside Road on July 23rd, 1955, heading the 2.20pm train from Gorgie East to Duddingston on the Edinburgh Suburban line. The normal formation for passenger trains on this line was five bogies, but this particular train only was restored for three./*A. Maclean*

ESKBANK & DALKEITH

Above right: Class J37 0-6-0 No 64552 of St

Margarets passes Hardengreen Junction on May 20th, 1960 with a southbound load of mineral 'bogeys'. The line to Galashiels via Peebles diverges to the left./*W. S. Sellar*

Right: Dalkeith station forms the background for J36 class 0-6-0 No 65344 as it rounds its train on the same day, having traversed the short branch from Glenesk Junction on the 'Waverley Route'./*W. S. Sellar*

NAVAL BASE JUNCTION

Above: Former North British Railway Class B 0-6-0 (LNER J35) heads a short freight train from Rosyth Dockyard to Inverkeithing past Naval Base Junction on Burntisland Control Area trip working 78. In the background can be seen the lattice work of the viaduct which carries the up line from Aberdeen to Edinburgh over the branch. The junction was installed in July 1912, and the signal box came into operation three months later. It was the point of convergence of the lines from Rosyth Dockyard and South Queensferry to Inverkeithing thence the Aberdeen main line. */Author's Collection*

KIRKCALDY & DYSART

Above right: To the south of Kirkcaldy lay the branch line across Fife to Auchtertool and Cowdenbeath. Built to prevent the Caledonian getting a foothold on the Fife coastline, the route was never opened to passenger traffic, although freight traffic started on March 3rd, 1896 and lasted until November 17th, 1963. Here, J37 class 0-6-0 No 64629 propels its brake vans from the down main line on to the branch on September 27th, 1960. */W. S. Sellar*

Right: Evening shadows are falling as BR Standard 2-6-0 No 76111 pulls away from Dysart with the second class only train which operated out with the public timetable between Thornton Junction and Rosyth Dockyard, outward in the morning, returning late afternoon. After the demise of steam, DMU cars undertook the working. */P. M. Westwater*

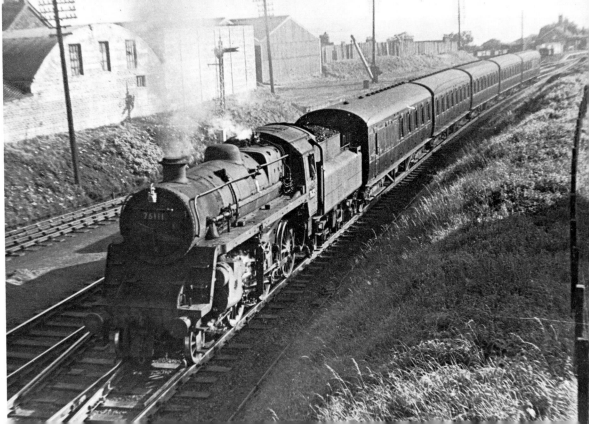

EAST FIFE

Above: In August 1965, one month before the line was closed, LNER Class B1 4-6-0 No 61342 leaves the single line section from St Andrews and enters Crail with a local train from Dundee to Glasgow (Queen Street). The class shared the final workings over the East of Fife Railway with the ubiquitous Diesel Multiple Unit./*C. Lawson Kerr*

Below: A line which was never to see a regular passenger service during its life was the 14¾ mile line from East Fife Central Junction to Lochty which was opened on August 21st, 1896. The scene at Lochty is captured here on February 18th, 1961 when Driver Graham and his mate took time out to pose beside their steed, the former NB 0-6-0 No 65345. This engine was one of the last two steam engines allocated to a Scottish Region shed, and the branch, after being lifted by British Rail was partially relaid privately for operation by no less a machine than a Gresley A4, becoming the first Scottish preserved working steam railway. In the print, 65345 stands almost on the site where the shed for 60009 *Union of South Africa* was to be erected./*W. S. Sellar*

D&A JOINT LINE

Originally built and operated as an independent railway company, the Dundee and Arbroath was taken over by the Caledonian before coming under the joint control with the NB in 1880.

Above: The terminal at Dundee East, with Class C16 4-4-2 No 67502 in charge of a down local service./ *W. S. Sellar*

Below: 67491 of the same class draws into West Ferry Station with another local. The former North British 4-4-2T locomotives were latterly quite intimately associated with the steam passenger trains over the line./ *W. S. Sellar*

MONTROSE

Top: LNER Class V2 2-6-2 No 60838 heads a down train of empty coaching stock over the fine viaduct at Montrose on July 4th, 1959./*W. A. C. Smith*

Above: A. Thompson B1 4-6-0 No 61146 draws into Montrose Station with the 12.40 pm from Glasgow express on the same day./*W. A. C. Smith*

WORMIT

Right: On May 28th, 1955, the 6.53 pm return Sunday School Excursion from Tayport to Dundee hauled by Class 5MT 4-6-0 No 45458 came to grief when the tender left the track inside the tunnel on the approach to Wormit Station. In the accident, three persons, one of whom was a child, lost their lives. This photograph taken only seconds after the wreckage came to rest shows the locomotive wreathed in steam and the leading four vehicles of the train with the passengers still inside. The leading two vehicles were of NB origin, the others visible, LNER/*BR*

NORTHERN REACHES

Top: Kinnaber Junction, focal point of the 'Railway Race to Aberdeen' is the location for Class V2 No 60973 at the head of the 11.00 am Glasgow (Buchanan Street) to Aberdeen service on August 8th, 1964./*W. A. C. Smith*

Above: The branch line from Montrose, northwards to Bervie marked the northernmost North British lines on the eastern side of the country. After the passenger service withdrawal on the branch in October 1951, the line was host to a daily freight train, and J37 class 0-6-0 No 64602 is seen on that working near North Water Bridge on May, 18th, 1966, three days before the final runs of all, ironically passenger workings on Sunday May 22nd./*W. A. C. Smith*

DUNFERMLINE LOWER

Above: North British Lower Quadrant signals give authority for LNER Class D49 4-4-0 No 62729, *Rutlandshire* to enter the station with a local train from Edinburgh of predominently LNER vehicles.

Below: LMS carriages behind LNER V2 2-6-2 locomotive No 60802 give the indication that the train standing in the down platform is for Perth and the north, via Kinross. The closure of the Kinross route in January 1970 robbed the station of a 'Main Line' status, being then served only by local DMU services from Edinburgh on an 'Outer Suburban' basis. / *Author's Collection*

THE DEVON VALLEY LINE

Above left: On August 24th, 1961, British Railways Standard Class '4MTT' No 80092 of Perth shed works a twin articulated set of coaches over the line, calling at Rumbling Bridge en route to Alloa./*D. Martin*

Left: No 80092 accelerates away from Tillicoultry on the return working. At this time, the branch was diesel worked, and the steam loco was covering a failure./*D. Martin*

Above: As if determined to obtain a sky backing at any cost for the Down Home at Rumbling Bridge, the NB placed it at a not inconsiderable height over rail. The absence of a ladder should be noted, the lamp being raised and lowered by crank handle at the base of the post. In this illustration, the signal is being approached by the 4.30 pm Perth to Glasgow Queen Street train on August 10th, 1957, made up of three LMS coaches with Class D34 No 62490 *Glen Fintaig* leading./*W. S. Sellar*

HYNDLAND BOUND

Top: J35 0-6-0 No 64468 (NB 856) passing Boghead Crossing, near Armadale West Lothian, with the 11.47 am Bathgate — Hyndland train on the last day of service, January 7th, 1956./ *W. A. C. Smith*

Above: Class N2 0-6-2T No 69564 near Maryville with

the 4.08pm Bothwell to Hyndland train on July 2nd, 1955./ *W. A. C. Smith*

With the coming of the Glasgow North Electric services, the terminus at Hyndland was closed, the name being transferred to a new station built on the electrified line between Partick Hill and Jordanhill/ Anniesland.

132

SINGER WORKERS TRAINS

Top: A large terminal station, never open to the general public but used for the workers of the Singer Sewing Machine Company in Glasgow, whose factory was adjacent, rejoiced in the name of the 'Singer Workers Platform'. In the view at the top, a varied array of motive power is present ready to cope with the homeward exodous from the factory, and features 2-6-2T 67618, 67625, and 67648. The ex-LMSR type is 2-6-0 No 43135. The date is August 26th, 1956./*W. A. C. Smith*

Above: J37 0-6-0 No 64639 Skirts the 'blocks' as it approached Springburn Station with a workers train from Singer via Maryhill on July 28th, 1960. 'The blocks' were banks of tenement houses built by the Edinburgh & Glasgow Railway for renting out to their staff, long before the practice had become widespread./*W. A. C. Smith*

BALLOCH PIER

Essentially an extension of the workaday line from Dumbarton to Balloch Central, the Pier station was a replacement of an earlier station named Balloch Wharf, the purpose of both of which was to serve the Loch Lomond Steamer Service. Operation was in the joint hands of the NB/Caledonian and later the LNE/LMS.

Below: LNER 2-6-2T No 67623 with the stock for a train for Bridgeton Cross (LNE)./*C. Lawson Kerr*

Bottom: A former Caledonian Railway 0-6-0 No 57554 with a rake of LMS stock for a Glasgow Central route service./*A. Maclean*

NORTH ELECTRIC (STEAM)

Above: Overhead wires are in position above Class J37 0-6-0 No 64574 as it arrives with a local train on August 2nd, 1960 at Helensburgh Central./*D. Martin*

Below: On November 7th, 1960, Electric Multiple Units completely supplanted steam over the former North British lines in the Glasgow Queen Street (Low Level) routes, but transformer difficulties forced the recall of the old warriors and on April 1st, 1961, V3 No 67618 is seen in heavy rain awaiting the departure signal from Airdrie with the 5.18pm to Anniesland./*W. A. C. Smith*

COWLAIRS INCLINE PILOTS

The NBR 0-6-2T locomotives of the '858' class (LNER N14) with one exception, were associated with the 1 in 45 Cowlairs incline throughout their service. The first of the class, as BR 69120 assists a passenger train up the incline in 1950./*N. E. Stead*

The development of the '858' type, although also classified 'A' by the NB became LNER class N15 and these engines, examples of which were built after 1923, found their way to most parts of the system. The one shown was fulfilling duties on the Pilot Working when photographed at Queen Street Station before taking a lift of empty coaches to the sidings at the summit in late 1959. Built in 1916, No 69181 survived until 1962./*A. Maclean*

Successors to the 'radial' tank engines of the N14 and N15 type were the Gresley 2-6-2T locomotives displaced from the Glasgow suburban routes by electrification. Here, No 67604 works hard at the rear of an Edinburgh train leaving Queen Street./*A. Maclean*

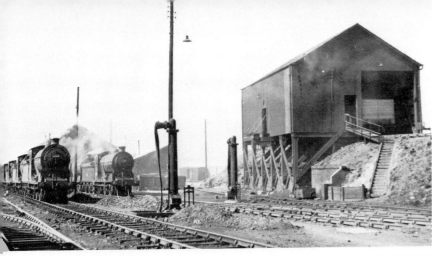

'ON SHED'

Seafield, sub shed of St Margarets, on the south side of the Firth of Forth on May 18th, 1958. All the engines are of NB origin, mainly of the large J37 type./*W. S. Sellar*

The west end of Haymarket Motive Power Depot in 1954 is the setting for this illustration, locomotives are, from top to bottom, D30 class 62437 *Adam Woodcock,* D11 class 62691 *Laird of Balmawhapple* and 62694 *James Fitzjames,* A2 class 60534 *Irish Elegance* and B1 No 61178./*Author's Collection*

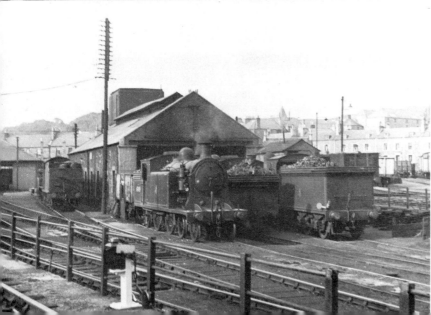

Sandwiched between the goods yard and goods shed lay the main depot at Hawick on the 'Waverley Route'. In this view of September 19th, 1955 the locomotive to the fore is 4-4-2T No 67489, with other NB engines alongside./*W. S. Sellar*

VIADUCTS & RAILTOURS

Above: The River Avon was crossed by more than one viaduct, and in this illustration Class N15 0-6-2T No 69163 heads a short train over the River between Bathgate and Avonbridge on May 6th, 1961./*W. S. Sellar*

Below: The most striking engineering feature on the 4¾ mile branch line from Markinch to Leslie, is this viaduct over the valley of the River Leven. The train is hauled by the preserved locomotive *Glen Douglas* and the date of the railtour was June 1962./*W. A. C. Smith*

STANDARD PACIFICS

Above: Clan class 4-6-2 No 72000 *Clan Buchannan* heads a troop special past the Edinburgh Suburban Station at Newington in August 1955, thus avoiding the congested lines through Edinburgh Waverley. The class was to number ten machines, but the proposed construction of a further ten was not carried out. 72000 was withdrawn in 1962, after a working life of only ten years./*A. Maclean*

Below: Britannia class locomotive No 70051, formerly named *Firth of Forth,* enters Glasgow Queen Street station with a Spring Holiday relief train from Edinburgh on April 18th, 1966./*S. Thompson*

DIESEL LOCOMOTIVES

Top: Introduced in 1958, the passage of time was to see all the Birmingham RC&W Type 2 Bo-Bo (Classes 26 and 27) allocated to former North British depots. Here D5355 brings an up Fort William to Glasgow train into Crianlarich Upper. On the West Highland, although trains call at every station, the North British practice of designating them as expressess still prevails./*A. Maclean*

Centre: A somewhat begrimmed 0-4-0 Paxman Hydraulic shunting locomotive No D2703 rests from shunting the freight yard at Polmont, adjacent to the Edinburgh & Glasgow main line./*A. Maclean*

Bottom: In 1926, Clayton 900 hp type 1 locomotives entered service from NB sheds. Here No D8578 is shown in Thornton Marshalling Yard with the first diesel hauled coal train for Kincardine Power Station on April 18th 1966. Never a popular design, they were destined to have a comparatively short life, all having gone from Scottish sheds by 1973./*A. Maclean*

DIESEL RAILCARS

Top: The first two sets of diesel railcars to operate in Scotland were of the Metropolitan Cammel twin unit type. One of the pair, E79055/79261 is depicted at the Edinburgh suburban terminus of Corstorphine in August 1956./*A. Maclean*

Centre: Derby Works built twin units had a brief operational spell in Scotland when new. Here, No M51424 leads on an Edinburgh Outer Circle service in 1959. The four character headcode was not used domestically in services based on Eastern Scottish depots./*A. Maclean*

Bottom: The first 'main line' DMU vehicles in Scotland were put to work in the Edinburgh & Glasgow service, gradually supplanting steam. In 1961, one set was regularly diagrammed across into Fife as a 'filling in' turn and in the illustration, is leaving the Forth Bridge at North Queensferry bound for Dunfermline on a local train./*BR*

EPITAPH TO STEAM

Above: The 1 in 43 gradient from Queen Street to Cowlairs in Glasgow forms the setting for this study in steam as A3 class 4-6-2 No 60096 *Papyrus* nears the summit with the 10.50 am Pullman train to London (Kings Cross), the 'Queen of Scots'. In the rear, a V1 2-6-2T adds its own quota of smoke and steam. The date is November 1961./*C. Lawson Kerr*

THOMPSON PACIFICS

Right: Class A2 Pacific No 60530, *Sayajirao* heads an up van train for the Dundee, Perth & London Shipping Company on the climb from Invekeithing through the Ferry Hills Cutting near North Queensferry in August 1965. Sister engine No 60532 *Blue Peter* has since been privately preserved as LNER 532, a style which she was not to carry in her working life./*C. Lawson Kerr*

142

WHEN DAY IS DONE

Former North British 0-6-0T locomotive No 68477 heads back to St Margarets Motive Power Depot in Edinburgh after completing its stint as Yard Pilot locomotive at Craigentinny Carriage Sidings./ *C. Lawson Kerr*